P O W E R I N G
I N C L U S I V E
C U L T U R E S

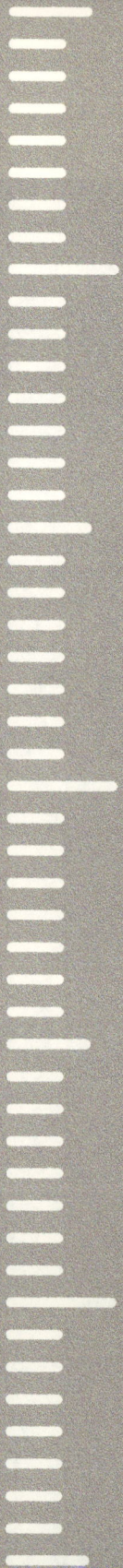

POWERING
INCLUSIVE
CULTURES

WHY
MEASUREMENT
MATTERS

CHRISTINE JONES

Advantage | Books

Published by Advantage Books, Charleston, South Carolina.
An imprint of Advantage Media.

ADVANTAGE is a registered trademark, and the Advantage colophon is a trademark of Advantage Media Group, Inc.

Printed in the United States of America.

10 9 8 7 6 5 4 3 2 1

ISBN: 978-1-64225-560-7 (Paperback)
ISBN: 978-1-64225-559-1 (eBook)

Library of Congress Control Number: 2023911837

Cover design by Lance Buckley.
Layout design by Lance Buckley.

This publication is designed to provide accurate and authoritative information in regard to the subject matter covered. It is sold with the understanding that the publisher is not engaged in rendering legal, accounting, or other professional services. If legal advice or other expert assistance is required, the services of a competent professional person should be sought.

Advantage Books is an imprint of Advantage Media Group. Advantage Media helps busy entrepreneurs, CEOs, and leaders write and publish a book to grow their business and become the authority in their field. Advantage authors comprise an exclusive community of industry professionals, idea-makers, and thought leaders. For more information go to **advantagemedia.com**.

Praise for *Powering Inclusive Cultures*

The book is easy to read and practical. It forces the reader to think about topics in a palatable way while also reassuring them that they are not alone. The stories really give colorful commentary to how organizations are experiencing DEI and seeing their way through. It has thoughtful insight as to how to approach DEI with the data to back it up!

—Tawana Bhagwat, CEO, Organization At Its Best

Leaders know that before embarking on any change, accessing the current situation is a must. The same is true when engaging in organizational or individual advancement of diversity, equity and inclusion. Chris Jones uses straight forward language, relatable stories and clear research-based recommendations that will help you access and then take actions toward achieving your DEI goals.

—Lenora Billings-Harris, Author, *Trailblazers: How Top Business Leaders are Accelerating Results through Inclusion and Diversity*

Small and medium sized organizations are competing for talent with large organizations. In that competitive world, having an inclusive and welcoming organization is a must have—not a nice to have. Powering Inclusive Cultures *is an excellent book to find out what needs doing in terms of diversity, equity and inclusion— and how to do it. Begin with measurement, so you can track your progress. Until then, you don't know what you don't know.*

—Julie Kratz, Author, *Allyship in Action*

I read a lot of books on DEI. What I really appreciated about this book are the learning activities which provide some really impactful aha moments. Spoiler alert ... did you know that "without diverse leadership, People of Color are 24 percent less likely than straight white men to win endorsements for their ideas?" I can see using the quizzes in each chapter as a great icebreaker for team meetings!

—LaJuana Warren, CEO Founder, Tapestry

In Powering Inclusive Cultures: Why Measurement Matters, *author Chris Jones showcases exemplary leadership by emphasizing the crucial role of statistically sound data and analysis as the foundation for effective diversity and inclusion initiatives. With a comprehensive exploration of various dimensions of diversity, this book provides a practical roadmap for organizations striving to build inclusive cultures that truly empower all individuals.*

—Amy C. Waninger, Author, *Lead at Any Level*

Till Jesse och Leila med vilkorslös kärlek.

(To Jesse and Leila, with unconditional love.)

CONTENTS

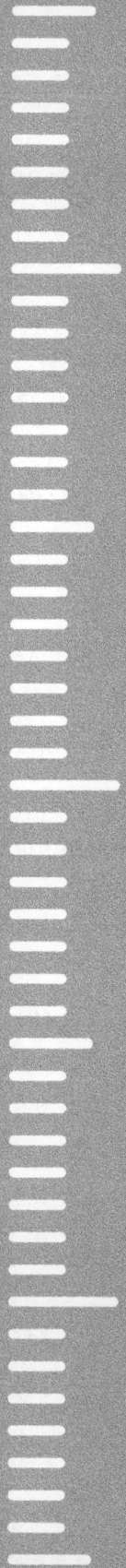

It ain't what you don't know that gets you into trouble.
It's what you know for sure that just ain't so.

—MARK TWAIN

Does This Ring a Bell?

If you're a CEO or C-suite executive, the idea of measuring diversity, equity and inclusion (DEI) in your organization may be the stuff of nightmares. I had one executive tell me flat out, "No way are we measuring ourselves. It would be awful." That may ring a bell for you. And you may think that bias training is the answer—even though it is rarely the solution.

DEI is a hot topic. The murder of George Floyd and the summer of Black Lives Matter protests brought diversity, equity and inclusion to the forefront. In a survey conducted in October of 2020, 96 percent of CEOs said that DEI was a top priority for them. Additionally, 90 percent put employee recruitment, development, advancement and retention as a strategic goal. As of this writing, executives seem to have cooled a bit in their interest in and commitment to DEI. The importance, however, remains unchanged.

As a CEO or C-suite executive, you have a valuable role in the continuum of DEI progress for your organization. In this book we'll show you why bias training alone doesn't work, and we'll give you tools that *will* work. This book is not about discrimination—which is already illegal and has been addressed in Equal Employment Opportunity Commission (EEOC) rulings and in many other ways. This book is about building resilience and outlines what it takes to move the DEI needle in a positive direction. You'll learn answers to questions like these:

- What is DEI, and why is it so hard?

- What techniques have proved effective beyond bias training?

- What have other companies done?

You may want to have a pen or pencil handy. The activities in this book will help you create muscle memory and internalize some of the lessons learned.

We also feature case studies from a variety of organizations to demonstrate what does and does not work. Let's start with an aviation museum.

CASE STUDY: Aviation Museum

If you knew nothing about aviation, you may think that an aviation museum includes the Wright brothers, Charles Lindbergh and possibly Amelia Earhart. That much is true. One museum's massive collection of aircraft is the story of male pilots, male astronauts (in the beginning), aircraft and wars. Their collection runs from the birth of flight through experimental aircraft to spaceflight.

However, some people and events were noticeably missing. For example, Ed Dwight was the first Black man to enter the air force training program from which NASA selected astronauts. He was forced to resign from NASA after making it all the way up to Phase II of training because America wasn't ready for a Black astronaut. There is no mention of him in the museum's exhibit on the Mercury program training. There are no books, movies or museum exhibits that tell his story.

Where does Ed belong in the history of aviation?

Another issue that concerned the museum was the demographic makeup of their staff and volunteers. They contacted my organization, Spectra Diversity, in 2019 and began with an assessment to collect their demographics and perceptions regarding management, culture and policies and practices and procedures.

Initially they thought they had a race issue. Maybe a gender issue. It turns out they had a generational issue. Their assessment results showed that employees who were twenty-five to thirty-four years old scored significantly lower than their older counterparts on organizational questions.

The assessment also captured responses to open-ended questions:

Do you have suggestions to foster more diversity and inclusion at our museum?

Are there instances of exclusion/noninclusion that you have experienced or witnessed at our museum?

Note that the museum was looking for the positive (ideas for the future) and the negative (examples of exclusion). Spectra Diversity's assessment, along with the results, enabled the museum to move forward in a positive and more inclusive direction.

Their open-ended responses included:

- Hire diverse populations for fundraising, education, exhibits, docents

- Tell a more inclusive story; the current collection is about things (aircraft, aviation, space)

- Approach wider group of people (underserved youth)

- Examine how different socioeconomic backgrounds affect behavior

- Be willing to be uncomfortable and see privilege

- Hold ourselves accountable for willful ignorance (we are white centric)

- Recognize that People of Color are burdened with the task of educating and guiding the majority.

As a result, the museum has:

- Created a DEI task council

- Conducted diversity and inclusion training for all staff and volunteers

- Revitalized exhibit spaces to be more inclusive of diverse stories

- Improved Americans with Disabilities Act (ADA) access in all areas

Kudos to the museum for beginning this work before others jumped on the great bandwagon which assembled worldwide after George Floyd's murder sparked a wave of protests against racial injustice.

The museum acknowledges what all of us should—that the goal of diversity, equity and inclusion is a journey and not a destination.

Their work continues.

Don't Be Afraid

Big organizations (3M, Target, Microsoft, etc.) have been working on diversity and inclusion (D&I) for decades. They have rooms full of D&I people. They have programs, training and systems in place. Even so—some of them make colossal boo-boos (a Starbucks story to illustrate this point will come later).

But what about small- and medium-size organizations? They may only have an HR person in charge of everything D&I related. They may have drafted an employee who happens to be Black, Asian American or another underrepresented group to oversee diversity and inclusion on top of whatever their regular job may be.

Since the pandemic began, we have witnessed the *great resignation*—a popular phrase referring to the thirty-three million people who left their jobs since the start of 2021. Considering these numbers, how can small organizations compete with bigger ones? Because compete they must. Since the summer of 2020, those of underrepresented races, ethnicities, gender identities, sexual orientation and abilities have had their eyes opened in a major way. There is no chance of unknitting that sweater or unringing that bell.

Employees everywhere have woken up. Taking a line from the movie *Network*, "I'm mad as hell, and I'm not going to take it anymore!"

Power versus Empower

The title of this book is intentional. It indicates what we're hoping you will do: power an inclusive culture at your organization. *Powering* and *empowering* are not synonyms, although they are often used interchangeably.

When you're *empowering* something (or someone), you're giving the authority or power to do something. It is a gift. You're in control of it until you give it away. This book isn't about empowering anyone. It's about powering an inclusive culture in your organization.

In contrast, when you're *powering* something, you're supplying energy. Powering is to move with great speed or force. Powering inclusion is generating it or fueling it. This book will show you how to do that. You will learn everything you need to know about powering an inclusive culture in your organization.

Multiple research studies show us the business case and benefits of diversity and inclusion.

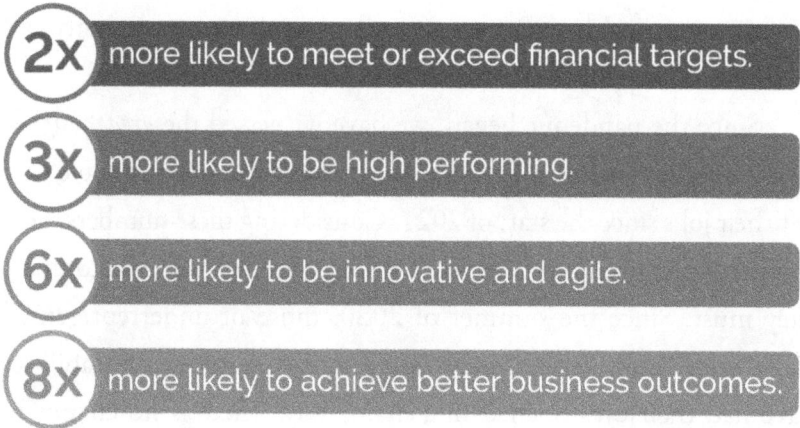

2x more likely to meet or exceed financial targets.

3x more likely to be high performing.

6x more likely to be innovative and agile.

8x more likely to achieve better business outcomes.

This begs the question: What happens to organizations that don't make diversity, equity and inclusion a priority in their organization?

Citi GPS (Global Perspectives and Solutions) released a report in September of 2020 titled "Closing the Racial Inequality Gaps," which speaks to the economic cost of Black inequality in the US.

CONSIDER THIS:

- Closing the Black wage gap could have added $2.7 trillion in income available for consumption or investment.

- Facilitating easy access to higher education for Black students could have increased lifetime incomes $90–$113 billion.

- Improving access to housing credit might have added an additional 770,000 Black homeowners, adding $218 billion in sales and expenditures.

- Providing fair and equitable lending to Black entrepreneurs might have resulted in the creation of an additional $13 trillion in business revenue and potentially created 6.1 million jobs per year.

If these racial gaps were closed today, we could see $5 trillion of additional GDP over the next five years, or an average add of 0.35 percentage points to US GDP growth per year and 0.09 percentage points to global growth per year. I highly recommend the Citi GPS report for further reading.

After the start of COVID-19 and the death of George Floyd, interest in DEI skyrocketed. Culture Amp's 2022 report, "Workplace Diversity, Equity & Inclusion Report: Understanding the DEI Landscape," surveyed 2,100 companies and a total of 1.1 million employees. One of the general trends discovered is that in 2021, 83 percent of employees felt that their company valued diversity, whereas only 72 percent of these same employees felt that their company builds diverse teams.

Not only are organizations failing to walk the talk, but they are also failing to put money where their public-facing mission statement is.

. . . .

"The leadership team can more effectively define diversity
and inclusion within the org and purposefully communicate
its importance to the team, as many beliefs are implicit
instead of explicit. On a personal level, we can better
equip managers to support team members who have
backgrounds different than their own and equip all team
members to work with people different than them."
—Anonymous[1]

. . . .

The time is now.

CEOs, C-suite executives and managers in any size of organization should begin their journey now. It doesn't have to break the bank to determine

- how you begin,

- where you stand now,

- what you can measure and what the results mean and

- how you can move forward.

This book is about powering your organization forward on the diversity, equity and inclusion journey, even—and especially—when you aren't sure where to begin.

---

[1] Anonymous real voices are people within the organizations Spectra Diversity has assessed. When you read them, imagine that these are your employees, because it is probable that people with these feelings and beliefs reside within your organization. How will you know—without measuring?

The Elephant in the Room

If you've looked at this book's cover, you can see that I'm a white woman. Not only that, but I'm a white cisgender baby boomer. As with the aviation museum, I've been on a journey of self-discovery, learning and making mistakes, combined with a passion to leave the world a better place than when I entered it. Think of my DEI experience as a learning journey rather than an experience journey.

My journey began with social activism (imagine a long-haired blond hippie, a Vietnam War protester). It moved into empathy when several of my close friends died of AIDS in the 1980s, when we didn't know what it was, how it was transmitted or whether there would ever be a cure. It continued with decades of letters to the editor, the Women's March in Washington, DC, in January of 2017 and protesting the separation of families at our southern border in 2018.

It also involved several mistakes. Here's one of them.

As a video producer during the 1980s, I was working on a video program about environmental sustainability for 3M. I imagined the video beginning with a voice-over quote from Chief Seattle as we see the leathery face of a Native American elder. Luckily for us, there was a stenographer in the audience when Chief Seattle gave many of his speeches (this excerpt is from one given in 1885), so we can remember his words as well as the man.

. . . .

"Will you teach your children what we have taught our children? That the earth is our mother? What befalls the earth befalls all the sons of the earth. This we know: the earth does not belong to man; man belongs to the earth. All things are connected like the blood that unites us all. Man did not weave the web of life; he is merely a strand in it. Whatever he does

to the web, he does to himself. One thing we know: our god
is also your god. The earth is precious to him and to harm the
earth is to heap contempt on its creator."

—Chief Seattle, 1885

. . . .

As a creative young producer, I thought I'd have a real live actor play the part of Chief Seattle. I contacted my local American Indian Movement (AIM) chapter and asked to connect to any actors who could play the part of Chief Seattle. I described my request, and the gentleman on the other end of the phone let out a deep sigh.

I was told very strongly, and politely, that I could not simply cast an Indian from our area to play Chief Seattle, who was a member of the Suquamish Tribe and Dkhw'Duw'Absh chief. The Twin Cities, Minneapolis and St. Paul, tribes included Chippewa, Ojibwe, Sioux and Lakota. They are totally different nations and not interchangeable at all without delivering a great insult. Needless to say, I have never made that mistake again.

As a white cisgender woman, I hold more privilege than many. Even so, I've been talked down to, talked over and ignored more than once.

One of my first "real" jobs, where I used my degree, was with the engineering firm Honeywell. Because I had a theater background, I was put in charge of the annual Engineering Night Banquet where the prestigious Sweatt Award was delivered. My budget at the time was somewhere just south of $200K, which was a lot of money in the '80s. I assembled my subject matter experts (engineers) for our first meeting. On that particular day, I forgot my secret clearance badge and was wearing a badge that read "Temp." As each engineer (all white men) strode into the room, I checked off their name and waited to begin. The gentleman next to me asked, "Are you here to take notes?"

"No," I replied. "I'm here to lead the meeting. Welcome, everyone…"

I left Honeywell in 1985 to branch out on my own as a consultant and video producer. One of the key elements of my work since then has been interviewing, on and off camera, a huge range of people. Those interview subjects include the CEO of 3M and other Fortune 500 organizations, rocket scientists at General Dynamics, the head of genetics at Mayo Clinic and polar explorer Ann Bancroft, to name a few. It also included people at a homeless shelter; women at a domestic-abuse service center; food-shelf volunteers; and rape survivors at Notre Dame, among other places. As an interviewer for more than thirty years, I've learned to listen carefully and without judgment. It's been a great honor to have so many people share their stories with me.

As time progressed, my role changed from international award-winning video producer and scriptwriter to multimedia producer, blogger and instructional designer. In my role as instructional designer, I began collaborating with colleagues in the diversity and inclusion field and worked on programs for large organizations including Verizon, Coca-Cola, Blue Cross Blue Shield and many others. I loved it. I was finally able to make a difference in some of the systemic issues present today.

Even so, being white in the diversity, equity and inclusion field comes with its own set of barriers. When I attempted to connect with a DEI professional on LinkedIn, I was told I "don't support white people commodifying oppression or taking on the lead in equity work. You haven't indicated there's a reason you're connecting with me which easily leads me to believe I'm being collected as a rare Indigenous equity professional. DEI is overtly still white centric, capitalistic and extremely colonial."

The consultant's statements about DEI professionals had a bit of truth to them. However, men can act as allies for women. Straight people can be allies for the LGBTQ community. And white people can certainly act as allies for the Black, Indigenous and People of Color (BIPOC) community.

We can all strive for inclusion and belonging. Diversity, equity and inclusion is a journey—not a destination.

What Was Missing?

As my colleagues and I continued working for these large companies, we began to notice some common patterns. How did we know that we were hitting the right target in our training? Were we off target? Was general knowledge enough? Could we change the individual and the leadership at the same time? What do we do about bias?

As a result, three of us formed Spectra Diversity and developed an assessment tool that measures both the individual and the organization in one assessment. It's statistically validated, which means that what we say it is measuring, it is in fact measuring. The results are not generated by chance. This is where you, dear leader or CEO, can begin your DEI journey—with measurement.

Whether it is the Spectra Assessment or one of the other well-known and authoritative assessments out there—measuring is key. Without measurement, you'll be at a serious disadvantage when developing a meaningful strategy to improve diversity, equity and inclusion within your organization.

Measurement Is Often the Missing Piece

Do your Black employees feel included? Are your women and men on the same page? Have you made a place for transgender employees at the table? Does your sales and marketing plan include People of

Color in the planning stages? How diverse is your board of directors, and why does it matter?

Data collected by measurements/assessments tells the story.

If you aren't measuring, you may not be effectively planning for the areas with the most need. For example, one of my colleagues was asked to do race training for an organization. She did an assessment and found the biggest disconnect was between generations. The baby boomers and the millennials were bumping heads. Had she gone in and strictly focused on race training (very beneficial in any case) without looking at generational issues, she might not have made as much of an impact.

Many questions can be answered with quantitative data—which is data that can be counted, like number of employees, number of women and number of branch offices. Many strategies can be developed with qualitative data—which is the data that cannot be counted, such as interview comments and employee suggestions.

**The *quantitative* (numbers) provides context
for the *qualitative* (comments).**

Some of the organizational strategies based on quantitative and qualitative data fall into a category I like to call *quick wins*. Others are more difficult, and we'll examine both in this book.

The key is to take the first step and not be afraid. CEOs, C-suite executives and managers need to be vulnerable to do this work, but it is worth it. Even a small shift can create big change within an organization. **It only takes 25 percent of a given population to create a positive change in that population.** The few can influence the many. You don't need everyone on board to improve DEI at your organization. But you no doubt need more than you have now!

That is the purpose of this book—to give you what you need now to move the DEI needle forward within your organization.

This book is organized to prepare you at every level to make those changes. Chapter 1 includes level setting about what DEI is and why it is important to you and to your employees. The chapters that follow focus on a key demographic (race/ethnicity, gender, sexual orientation, age, ability and veteran status) and explore how perspectives differ from the primary demographic in each area. We'll look at how each group views management; organizational culture; and the policies, practices and procedures that tend to hold the status quo in place. The final chapter looks at the different ways you can *power* your DEI efforts so we can all head toward a more diverse, equitable and inclusive world.

Let's begin with a closer look at DEI data and the story it tells.

KEY INSIGHTS

❏ Don't be afraid. As CEO or leader, you're used to tackling the tough stuff. This is one of those times.

❏ Diversity, equity and inclusion can be your strategic advantage for employee recruitment and retention. Use it.

❏ Start now. As a country, we are becoming more diverse by the minute. Get a wiggle on and start moving.

CHAPTER 1

Where to Start?

*The most difficult thing is the decision to act, the
rest is merely tenacity. The fears are paper tigers.
You can do anything you decide to do.*

—AMELIA EARHART

Start with Coffee: Learn from the Mistakes of Others

CASE STUDY: Starbucks

On April 12, 2018, two Black men in a Philadelphia Starbucks waited to meet a third man. One of the two men was told he couldn't use the restroom since he hadn't purchased anything. The employee/manager then approached the pair's table to ask if the two customers needed any help, which they declined. Next, the barista called the authorities. When five police arrived and arrested the two men, a Starbucks patron recorded the arrest. What happened next was every CEO's nightmare.

- April 13: Video went viral

- April 14: Starbucks CEO issued an apology via Twitter

- April 15: Announced implicit bias training

- May 11: Changed policy to allow nonpaying customers to use the restrooms

- May 29: Closed all stores in the afternoon to conduct implicit bias training

To many in the diversity, equity and inclusion field, the decision to close the stores seemed like a move designed to change the Starbucks image rather than to change behavior. It was a knee-jerk reaction. Luke Visconti, CEO of DiversityInc, believes the move was too fast.

> "If there was a problem with the temperature of the milk used to put in coffee, it would take them longer to study the problem than six weeks, and they wouldn't hire celebrities (Eric Holder?) in an attempt to give them credibility. The speed at which they are doing this says to me that this is a PR reaction. But it's not a PR problem. As evidenced by the poor human capital results on their own corporate leadership page (57 people pictured, 19 women, three Blacks, no apparent Latinxs), the corporate culture needs to be repaired from the head down—as it does for all strategic business problems."

Not only did Starbucks demonstrate a knee-jerk reaction, but it was also pretty much guaranteed not to work. The coffeehouse company could have learned a few lessons from organizations that have been working on these issues for more than forty years.

"There should be more training of the staff, especially supervisors and managers, in diversity and inclusion. This should
be continuous and if possible one of the required trainings
for the annual evaluation of staff."

—Anonymous

Why Diversity, Equity and Inclusion Matters in Organizations

The focus of this book is on **diversity** (how you hire), **equity** (how you pay and promote) and **inclusion** (how you keep people) within the United States. These terms are often used together, although they have distinctly different meanings and impacts within an organization. We'll look at that in more depth in this chapter. Any organization's diversity, equity and inclusion work is a journey that is traveled, not a destination to reach. The journey from diversity through to equity and inclusion is a long one, with a few "historical milestones" along the way. One such milestone is the US Civil Rights Act.

In 1964, the Civil Rights Act made it illegal for organizations to engage in employment practices that discriminated based on race, color, religions, gender, national origin, age and disability. In 1965, Executive Order 11246 was passed, requiring all government contractors to take affirmative actions to overcome past patterns of exclusion and discrimination.

Formal diversity training began in the 1970s, following the civil rights era, in response to a social justice movement focused on race and gender.

In the 1980s, many organizations began by working on diversity. They made attempts to hire for diversity, which in most cases meant People of Color. There's much more to diversity, however. There is the diversity we see (skin color, hijabs, wheelchairs, gray hair) and the diversity we *don't* see (PTSD, mental health, neurodiversity, class).

Today, the business case for diversity is driven by the belief that a more diverse workforce produces better results and has a positive impact in the marketplace. Having a diverse workforce is important, but companies have realized that workplace culture must also be inclusive. Organizations that are most successful in creating a diverse and inclusive culture often link and integrate DEI to the organization's core-values mission and business objectives. Many focus on the importance of having cultural competence as an important skill domestically, as well as in the global arena. Cultural competence can be defined as the ability to understand, appreciate and interact with people from cultures or belief systems different from one's own.

Achieving diversity and inclusion requires intentional efforts and a strong commitment of senior leadership.

What is diversity? The presence of differences that make each person unique.

Think of diversity as an iceberg. Much of what we see as diversity is above the surface (race, ability, age, gender), but much of what constitutes diversity is below the surface. Sara Taylor, founder of deepSEE Consulting describes diversity as "differences that may make a difference."

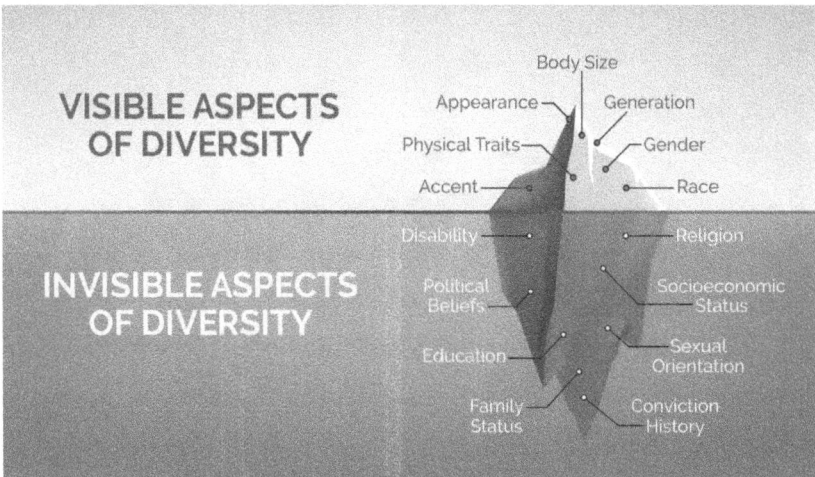

Diversity, a collection of similarities and differences that we each carry with us, is based upon

- characteristics we were born with,

- experiences we have had and

- choices we have made.

What is equity?
An approach to ensure everyone has
access to the same opportunities.

Equity increased in importance when organizations and their employees realized that the golden rule no longer fit. Treating others as you wish to be treated does not take into consideration that other people from other backgrounds or cultures don't necessarily see the world as you do or need the same things that you do. Follow instead the platinum rule and **treat others as they themselves wish to be treated**.

A colleague of mine gives this as an example of not everyone wishing to be treated "equally."

I was in a business meeting with an African American client and a Hispanic colleague. At the end of the meeting, those two hugged. I thought we were all a team, so I leaned in for my hug. My Hispanic colleague quickly intervened to help me "save face." It was too early in the relationship, and I was assuming familiarity too quickly. As a Caucasian female, I have learned to take a step back and watch the cues from others instead of making assumptions. I still have to pull myself back and remember I have to earn that respect and relationship.

In Hispanic cultures, relationship is one of the paramount values from which they operate, whereas white people in the US are typically task oriented. When I was in Thailand, I noticed their preference for harmony and collectivism, or importance of the group rather than the individual. Asian cultures have an indirect conflict style (saving face) by not taking part in direct confrontation. For example, in Thailand, there's no such word as *no*. Rather than saying no directly, people might say "Maybe" or "Not yet." Even *yes* doesn't always mean yes. In Asian cultures, yes might mean "Yes, I heard you" rather than "Yes, I agree with you."

Treating people the same doesn't always work when they come from different cultures, even if both were raised in the US.

Not everyone needs the same thing. Neurodiverse people may need an office with a door. People of certain religions may need a place to say their daily prayers. Making an accommodation for one person doesn't mean it needs to become a company policy. Starting pay may need to be a specific amount rather than a range because men tend to inflate their worth when being hired and women tend to minimize. The gender wage-income gap grows larger each year when the starting salary begins at different levels.

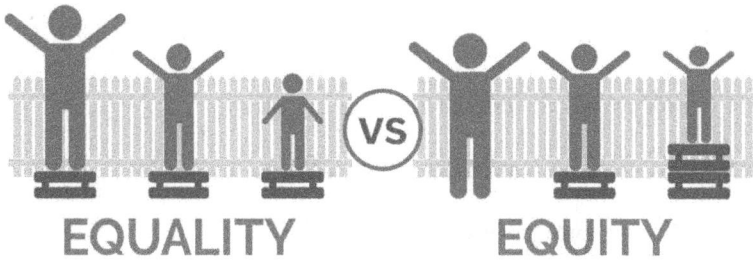

To reap the fruits of life, some people can stand on their own two feet, some people may need a little stool, and a third person may need a ladder or to stand on someone's shoulders. As the above image illustrates, equality and equity are not the same thing.

Equality can relate to accommodations, but it can also equate to a state of being considered equal. In that instance, it is something for which we can strive. So you and I are equal in the eyes of the law.

Recently the word *justice* has been added to *DEI* to become *JEDI*. There is something magical about the thought of swinging a lightsaber as a JEDI knight against the chains of social injustice. However, that is beyond the scope of this book. The systemic injustice we will be examining here is the systemic racism, sexism and other isms present within an organization. To repeat, our focus is on diversity (how you hire), equity (how you pay and promote) and inclusion (how you keep people).

What is inclusion?
The full engagement and development of all employees.

Diversity became a focal point in popular culture in the 1960s during the civil rights era. Later it was discovered, through trial and error, that diversity wasn't enough. An organization had to include everyone—and create a sense of belonging—or their newfound diverse employees would walk out the door.

Those who are diverse and not feeling included may

- look or feel different from the majority,

- minimize or maximize traits to fit in,

- seek acceptance of ones' true self,

- disengage when not feeling seen or heard or

- quit or leave because they feel they don't belong.

Inclusion is an experience. In the US we've been led to believe that we are a great melting pot and that, eventually, we all become part of the universal soup of our culture. In reality, we are more like a tossed salad. In a tossed salad, the individual fruits, nuts or vegetables retain their taste and shape. They exist next to each other. Some of the ingredients are permeable and soak in the dressing (croutons), while others treat the dressing as a separate flavor which they will carry forward without changing their own texture and flavor (grapes). Think of your organization as a tossed salad. Inclusion is an experience—and those who do not experience inclusion will leave eventually.

Consider this: companies spend $200 billion on advertising, $500 billion on research and development and $6 trillion on employees (hiring, training, rehiring and retraining). If you're working to improve your organization, you may pour money into the sales, marketing or product-development bucket—although the bucket that can have the most impact *on* those other buckets is the employee bucket. The employee bucket holds employee training, salaries, benefits and other aspects that affect employee engagement and a feeling of belonging.

Paolo Gaudiano, president of Aleria Research Corporation, chief scientist at Aleria and adjunct associate professor at the NYU Stern

School of Business had this to say at the 2022 Diversity & Inclusion Research Conference:

"The inevitable conclusion is that for virtually every organization, people are the most valuable asset and the most expensive budget item. Learning to 'diversify human assets' through DEIB [diversity, equity, inclusion, belonging] can be the most competitive advantage of any organization."

—Paolo Gaudiano

Benefits and Challenges

"When other coworkers and myself have brought up feeling uncomfortable due to sexist and racist behavior of coworkers and volunteers, we were told to deal with it because we were not supposed to make the other party uncomfortable. I was literally told that we did not want the other party to feel like they were 'walking on eggshells.' In turn I was left to feel I was 'walking on eggshells.'"

—Anonymous

When I have a difficult choice to make, I often start with a list of pros and cons. If you were to do that with the benefits and risks of diversity, equity and inclusion, your list would certainly include these proven benefits.

Here are some benefits of DEI for an organization:

1. DEI helps employees feel safe, respected and connected.

2. DEI efforts help employees feel a sense of belonging.

3. Inclusion can help combat "work-from-home burnout."

4. Diverse employees can reach a wider audience.

5. DEI efforts can be connected to a company's values.

6. Inclusion creates a sense of psychological safety.

7. Increased empathy translates to increased team building.

8. A diverse, inclusive environment retains employees.

Most of the benefits come with positive financial results. If you were to consider the downside of DEI efforts, your list might look a little different.

Some DEI challenges:

1. Those in power may feel uncomfortable. It is hard to acknowledge one's white male privilege, for example. However, consider that white men account for 72 percent of corporate leadership at sixteen of the Fortune 500 companies.

2. Organizations may be change resistant. However, change is part of life. Gone and liquidated are Lord & Taylor, Pier 1 Imports, Toys "R" Us, Borders Books, Circuit City, Blockbuster and many more. In some cases, they weren't quick enough to change with the times (innovation) or didn't keep up with their (diverse) customers' needs.

3. DEI assessments and strategies cost money. Why should you invest in DEI (i.e., your employees)? Because employee investments improve productivity, improve your bottom

line, improve employee retention and reduce turnover. A penny spent and a dollar earned.

4. DEI work can expose sexism, homophobia, racism, classism, ableism, anti-Semitism and ageism. Isms can flourish in darkness and can wither and die when exposed to the light. DEI work can force them into the open, which is a vulnerable place to be.

5. If a chief diversity officer is hired, that individual will need to be skilled at conflict resolution. Bringing different people together naturally creates conflict when dealing with those who are the "other" (and not "us").

Assuming you've decided to give DEI work a try, your first impulse may be to hire someone to do implicit or unconscious bias training.

Does Implicit Bias Training Work?

The usual playbook for improving diversity, equity and inclusion involves one-off antibias training, compliance assessments, annual engagement surveys and other efforts that ultimately don't work or are not properly targeted or validated. Implicit or unconscious bias training seeks to uncover our hidden biases so we can prevent them from getting in the way of inclusive behavior.

A proactive organization will conduct interviews and focus groups, but these rarely give a full picture of the state of an organization's position on the DEI journey without statistical data (numbers) to accompany the qualitative data (comments). Some leaders might hire a diversity officer and leave it to them to turn around an organization's entire culture. Even more common is to recruit a person of color within the organization and assign them the DEI task—even though they are not trained in this field.

There are two problems with the adoption of unconscious bias training as a first step.

1. Without measurement first, you may not have accurately identified your DEI issues.

2. Implicit (unconscious) bias training doesn't work as a stand-alone solution.

Based on the data Spectra Diversity has collected, there are several common issues faced by small- and medium-size businesses. It is common that an organization's leaders believe the issue to be with one demographic—only to find out that fewer positive perceptions are held by another group.

Another common result is that the C-suite or top leaders often view their own organization through rose-colored glasses. Our data show that they believe they're doing better on the DEI metrics compared to what their employees believe.

Implicit Bias Training Doesn't Work: Here's Why

The first and natural reaction of many after the killing of George Floyd, Breonna Taylor and Ahmaud Arbury may have been "Oh my gosh—we need to do something! Let's get some bias training in here!" Bias training became the hot activity, resulting in more than $8 billion spent annually, according to McKinsey & Company.

Here are a few reasons why unconscious bias training as a stand-alone effort does not work.

Mandatory Unconscious (Implicit) Bias Training Can Incite Anger

Those who don't really believe in the basic premises of diversity, equity and inclusion become even more resistant when unconscious bias training is mandatory. Not only that, but they can also become the proverbial rotten apple and influence others in the training to either clam up (freeze), check out (flight) or lash out (fight). You want any training you do to be effective, right? Unconscious bias training can cause resistance among those who need it most—white cisgender able-bodied men. Also, any training taking place needs to happen in a place of trust.

Our Biases Short-Circuit Our Brains

Our implicit or unconscious biases have been forming and reforming since we were very young children. Those are old, well-worn and patterned grooves in our brain circuitry. Our brain reacts one way, even though our mind is thinking or believing another. This is the *intent-action gap*. Specifically, the intent-action gap refers to the gap between a person's intent to behave a certain way and their ability to act accordingly. Why? Because of unconscious processes that hijack decision-making.

Think about it in terms of breaking a habit. You may know you need to lose weight by eating right and exercising at least a minimum amount. That's your intent. But do you do that? Quite often the answer is no. That is the action—or lack thereof. The problem with weight in the US indicates that many of us have an intent-action gap. I am guilty as charged.

Focus Is Misplaced on the Individual Rather than the Systems

Imagine DEI is an Olympic sport. Everyone is competing for the highest scores in an event. However, one country has better equipment, early access to the training ground and more judges from the home country than the other teams. None of those things can be controlled or influenced by an individual. In the DEI space, a single line-level employee would have a hard time changing the hiring procedures, promotions, pay scale or diversity makeup of the board of directors. System changes require intent and action at the top. Focus on the systems first—and then the individuals.

Look at systemic change rather than individual change.

Tidal Equality, a Canadian strategy firm at the intersection of social change and diversity and inclusion gives three more reasons why unconscious bias training doesn't work.

The Belief That Meritocracy Works

Meritocracy is a fallacy. How many times have you heard that "others" just need to pull themselves up by their bootstraps? Work harder and you'll be rewarded. Our organization hires and promotes fairly. Sadly, studies show that this simply is not the case. For example, women are graduating with STEM degrees on par with men. However, seven years after graduation, 83 percent of those women have left their STEM careers.

Implicit Bias Training Justifies Biased Decision-Making

Have you seen the television commercial for Sling TV where a food server slips on the floor and a patron jumps up and claims to know how to provide first aid because she's watched a lot of medical programs?

28

"Don't worry—her kidneys are still beating," says the patron. What happens after unconscious bias training is that people who completed the half day or full day of training are overconfident in their abilities. The opposite is true. Those who have completed unconscious bias training can, in terms of stereotyping, get worse instead of better.

Just Talking about Stereotypes Can Lead to Stereotype Confirmation

Discussing stereotypes is a tough conversation, and it's why unconscious bias training is best left in the hands of an experienced professional. Studies have shown that when stereotypes are mentioned, the brain, a very efficient learner, will collect the information about the stereotype and will *confirm* the stereotype rather than disavow it.

By now you might have guessed that Starbucks's approach might not have been effective. What could they have done instead, and why does measurement matter? Consider this: What do organizations that have been working on diversity, equity and inclusion since the 1980s teach us?

The Need for Real Change

It is our contention that to make real change, you need to begin with real information. You must measure real numbers with quantitative data and real stories with qualitative data.

CASE STUDY: Starbucks Part Deux

Resuming our Starbucks story, as of this writing, Starbucks leadership is fighting, somewhat unsuccessfully, to keep the union out of their stores. Starbucks CEO Howard Schultz returned to lead the company on an interim basis to right the ship. Starbucks partners at more than two hundred stores across the US have filed a petition to unionize, and twenty-six locations have achieved confirmed union vote victories (with two voting against unionization).

I've had two personal experiences with union membership, starting with the Meat Cutters union, which I joined so I could cashier at a grocery store. As far as I could see, the only thing this union did for me was take part of my paycheck. The second union was the Hotel Employees and Restaurant Employees Union. When the restaurant where I was waitressing expected me to pick up the tab for a table that did a "dine and dash" (eating and leaving without paying), this union not only helped me avoid paying that bill but also saved my job.

Unions have been around longer than many people may realize and developed out of workers striking for fairness (equity) in the workplace. The first strike occurred in 1768, when New York journeymen tailors protested a wage reduction. The first union was formed a few years later by shoemakers in Philadelphia. The formation of the Federal Society of Journeymen Cordwainers was founded in 1794. Since then,

- 34.8 percent of the workforce belonged to a union (in 1954).

- 14.7 million wage and salary workers were part of a union (in 2018).

- ▫ 25 percent were women

- ▫ 28 percent were Black or African American

- 10.8 percent of the US workforce belonged to a union (in 2019).

Workplace fairness, equity and inclusion are still present in many of today's unions and unionization efforts. At the same time, many unions have a checkered past, with internal inequities and corruption.

The great resignation has drawn a stark difference between CEO pay and what frontline employees are paid. Starbucks CEO Kevin Johnson's total compensation last fiscal year was about $13.4 million, or approximately 1,049 times the $12,754 the coffee giant's median employee earned in pay and stock.

Starbucks has been on a rocky road in terms of employee benefits and other factors. In 2019, Starbucks fired two Philadelphia baristas who were trying to unionize their stores, killing the effort before it had even started and drawing a rebuke from a National Labor Relations Board judge that ruled the company had violated the workers' rights.

Here is Starbucks's to-do list, published in 2020.

- We will launch a mentorship program connecting Black, Indigenous and People of Color (BIPOC) partners to senior leaders, beginning with a cohort of svp+ leaders and BIPOC directors in corporate and retail roles in FY21.

- We will invest in strategic partnerships with professional organizations that focus on the development of BIPOC talent, providing additional development opportunities for our BIPOC partners.

- We will partner closely with the Black Partner Network, Hora del Café, India Partner Network, Indigenous Partner Network and Pan-Asian Partner Network to better understand and support the experiences of our BIPOC partners.

- We will invest in additional Partner Network development and recognition programs across all networks, including an Inclusion and Diversity Virtual Leadership Summit in Q2 FY21.

- We will create foundational Inclusion and Diversity learning modules for US-based partners.

- We will embed antibias content into all hiring, development and performance assessment tool kits.

- We will enhance tools for our retail partners to improve internal talent advancement and opportunity in US retail. We will introduce a new Applicant Tracking System to help view promotion opportunities and for partners to express interest in open roles.

Starbucks seems to have made some progress—although not enough to satisfy workers. The grassroots unionization movement had spread via Instagram and Twitter and by mid-February 2021 had grown to ninety-eight stores in thirty states, including Rochester, NY; Kansas City, MO; Santa Cruz, CA; Eugene, OR; Tallahassee, FL; and Everett, WA. The first unionized store was in Buffalo, New York.

Starbucks is raising prices after reporting a 31 percent increase in profits. The company's revenue increased by almost 20 percent to over $8 billion. Their CEO's pay increased by almost 40 percent last year to more than $20 million.

The Moral of the Story

Union participation is increasing nationwide. Your organization may not be facing unionization of its workers; however, consider why employee unions are needed or created in the first place.

- Worker safety

- Better pay (equity)

- Better family leave benefits (inclusion)

- Time off for mental health (inclusion)

Organizations that measure regularly and have their finger on the pulse of their employees in terms of diversity, equity and inclusion can progress and thrive in the post-COVID-19 world.

One such company is Life Time Fitness.

Measure First, Then Strategize

CASE STUDY: Life Time

Life Time, the nation's premier healthy-way-of-life brand (NYSE: LTH), has approximately thirty thousand employees. Unlike Starbucks, Life Time measured before problems raised their ugly little heads.

Their DEI journey began in 2017. I spoke with David Pettrone Swalve, senior vice president, workforce inclusion and learning development at Life Time Inc. Swalve said,

We were in discovery mode at that time with the goal of understanding the basis of our performance and culture at Life Time. We conducted research and discovery in 2017,

2018 and 2019 in collaboration with McKinsey & Company, Graduate School of Business at Stanford University and Ross School of Business' Executive Education Program at the University of Michigan. Through this, we discovered the need to raise the bar for inclusion, equity and diversity and the tremendous importance of doing so.

According to Swalve, The Diversity Bonus, *by Scott Page, was a helpful resource.*

The concept of EI ID (equity drives inclusion and inclusion creates diversity) drove our evolution. It was the acknowledgment that when you make a team member feel respected, welcomed and valued to fully participate, you're going to benefit and achieve differential participation.

They created their own assessment and measured the organization in 2020.

Through team member feedback, we discovered the need to increase our intentionality in this area, so it wasn't seen as "soup du jour" or the topic of the month. Not only did we need to formalize and articulate our commitment, but we also needed to ensure all team members had the opportunity to have shared impact in the workplace and feel a genuine sense of inclusion or belonging. Moreover, by developing more inclusive leaders, we took steps to ensure they understood the capabilities—and responsibilities—of an inclusive leader. Through curiosity, conscious courage, commitment, collabo-

ration and cultural intelligence we developed stronger leaders, positively impacting our DEI assessment results over time.

Since Life Time's initial assessment, the organization has

- launched a formal mentoring program,

- implemented a dedicated EI ID learning curricula (and infused inclusion leadership into leader development),

- launched an executive coaching initiative,

- expanded the healthy-way-of-life community to those who live beyond our physical reach—for more equitable community access to a healthy way of life,

- closely monitored the employee sociodemographic categories and

- launched a charter inclusion council with ambassadors at each Life Time location.

In addition, their data revealed insights to help them create a more comprehensive definition of their best performers.

We're increasing our representation of diverse leaders and women leaders in our organization by 20 to 30% a year. We're taking away bias and prejudice and saying, "Hey, let's look more at merit and performance." When you look through this lens, the results are incredibly impactful in analyzing future leaders and culture in general.

The organization also has shared its progress in this area via communication with all employees and continues to reinforce it in leadership sessions and dedicated training. Swalve concluded,

If you're driven by the same thing I'm driven by, which is ultimately that our stakeholders, shareholders and investors concern themselves with both our EBITDA (Earnings Before Interest, Taxes, Depreciation and Amortization) and our profit, fully embracing and activating DEI at the foundational level is equally critical as employees, customers and key stakeholders prioritize organizations who value and uphold it.

LEARNING ACTIVITY

How Much Do You Know? (Answers in Appendix)

We're going old-school here. Please match the statement in the left column with the percentage or other number in the right column. Draw a line in the book connecting the statement with the number.

The multiracial population was measured at 9 million people in 2010 and 33.8 million people in 2020, a ____ percent increase.

129

The "Some Other Race" alone or in combination group (49.9 million) increased ____ percent, surpassing the Black or African American population (46.9 million) as the second-largest race alone or in combination group (compared to white/Caucasian).

276

In a study of 506 US-based businesses, each ____ percent increase in the rate of gender diversity resulted in an approximately 3 percent increase in sales revenues, up to the rate represented in the relevant population.

41

Sixty-one million adults in the United States live with a disability. ____ percent of adults in the United States have some type of disability.

1

In 2018, women earned 44.7 percent of master's degrees and ____ percent of doctoral degrees.

26

ACTION ITEMS

❑ Learn from the mistakes of others. You don't need to reinvent the DEI wheel. Follow the leaders.

❑ Measure first. Without measurement, you may travel unknowingly down a dead-end path.

❑ Work on inclusion. Diversity means little without inclusion.

❑ Act now. Underrepresented groups have lost patience. DEI changes must happen or you'll lose good people.

❑ Do more than unconscious bias training. Stand-alone training can harm more than help.

CHAPTER 2

Are You Measuring What Matters?

Every line is the perfect length if you don't measure it.

—MARTY RUBIN

Walking the Talk

By now you could be realizing that your organization has work to do—and you may not know all that you do not know. Fear not! When you measure what matters, you discover your organization's strengths as well as weaknesses. When you measure what matters, you are putting *power* behind your inclusive culture strategies.

Here is a short four-question assessment to check your organizational knowledge compared to other small- and medium-size businesses. Rate your organization on a scale of 1 (strongly disagree) to 5 (strongly agree). The average ranking answers are in the appendix.

YOUR RANKING (1–10)	AVERAGE RANKING (OTHER SMBS)	SURVEY STATEMENT
		I understand what diversity, equity and inclusion mean.
		Management has created a culture of diversity, equity and inclusion.
		Management shows that diversity is important through their actions.
		Effort is made to solicit ideas from all employees.

Do you think your employees would answer those questions the same way you just did? What about your Black employees? Do your male and female and transgender employees agree? If you agree to measure, you may have your eyes opened to strengths you have as well as some potential shortcomings.

CASE STUDY: ASHI

The American Society for Histocompatibility and Immunogenetics (ASHI) is a case in point because the team learned some surprising news.

A little background information:

- Histocompatibility is compatibility between the tissues of different individuals, so that one accepts a graft from another without having an immune reaction.

- Immunogenetics is a branch of immunology concerned with the interrelations of heredity, disease and the immune system and its components.

ASHI is an international society of professionals dedicated to advancing the science, education and application of immunogenetics and transplant immunology. Their vision is to be the foremost authority and leading educational resource in immunogenetics and histocompatibility. They seek to improve the quality of human life and health through the translation and implementation of scientific innovations to clinical practice.

When ASHI conducted their DEI assessment, they received surprising news. There was virtually *no difference* in the way employees, regardless of gender, viewed the three organizational categories measured by the Spectra Assessment (management, culture and the three Ps—policies, practices and procedures).

This is highly unusual. They were very proud of this fact and communicated it to their employees and association members. This good news can be used in employee and member recruitment as an example of fairness, equity and inclusion.

ASHI leadership is walking the talk.

Why Measure?

You learned in chapter 1 about the intent-action gap. If you were on a weight-loss program, you could measure the results of your action in several ways: your bathroom scale (quantitative data) or comments you receive, such as "Have you lost weight?" (qualitative data). The same holds true for your DEI survey.

Assessment Types in the World Today

It's important to draw a distinction between adding a few items on your annual employee satisfaction or engagement survey rather than a DEI survey. For one, they aren't the same thing.

Satisfaction: A satisfied employee could be one who likes the pay, the short commute and the friends they've made at the office. The satisfied employee may not be a high performer but is no doubt a loyal employee. They care about their fellow employees.

Engagement: An engaged employee could be one of your high performers, who always asks for career-stretching projects and is a high-output employee. They may also be learning as much as they can at your organization and will jump ship at the earliest opportunity. They care about themselves—not the organization.

Inclusion: The inclusive employee recognizes the value of diversity, equity and inclusion. They are a team player and often a role model. If they are not in an underrepresented group, they are an ally to those who are. They care about the organization and all its employees.

Self-Assessment Profiles: You may have taken the Myers-Briggs (personality) or DiSC (communication styles) assessments in the past. These self-assessments give you a profile of where you are in relation to others. Similarly, the Spectra Assessment includes a report on an individual's beliefs and interpersonal skills related to DEI, as well as

42

a ranking on the Spectra Diversity five-stage Maturity Model. The IDI (intercultural development inventory) provides a profile of the individual's ranking on a five-scale model (denial, polarization, minimization, acceptance and adaptation).

If You Measure, It Will Improve

On balance, research suggests that self-assessments contribute to higher achievement and improved behavior. The University of Toronto reported that "the psychometric properties of self-assessment suggest that it is a reliable assessment technique producing consistent results across items, tasks and contexts and over short time periods." Students with greater confidence in their ability to accomplish a targeted task were more likely to visualize success than failure. This caused them to set higher standards of performance for themselves. Student expectations about future performance could thereby influence effort.

There's a saying in carpentry: measure twice, cut once. The idea is to avoid an expensive mistake by making sure your measurements are accurate. The same is true for DEI programs. The only way to see the whole DEI picture is to measure it.

And if you don't "measure twice," you could focus your efforts on the wrong issue. There are several different diversity dimensions—age, race, gender identity and sexual orientation, for example. Even within these groups, there are social factors such as political beliefs, income and marital and parental status.

If you'd like to make DEI improvements within your organization, don't try a few strategies and then measure. Measure right away using the Spectra Diversity Inclusion Assessment or other validated measurement tool. The simple fact that you measure may improve your employees' interpersonal skills and beliefs related to DEI.

What to Measure?

Assume at this point that we've convinced you of the need to measure to make DEI progress. Yay! There are many DEI and culture surveys out there. Here's what the Spectra Assessment measures:

For individuals:

- Beliefs—self-awareness and personal beliefs around diversity, equity and inclusion

- Interpersonal skills—putting inclusion into action

For the organization:

- Management—how management sees itself and how employees see management

- Culture—organizational norms and beliefs

- Policies, practices and procedures (three *P*s)—how DEI is put into practice

Like attracts like, so if your business wants to attract certain demographic groups, focus on hiring within those groups. For example, diversity of opinion is not hiring from both Harvard and Yale. It is hiring from Ivy League schools, historically Black colleges and universities (HBCUs), Hispanic-serving institutions, tribal colleges, state schools and community colleges. You could even consider people without a degree who have shown they have the relevant experience. Bill Gates was a college dropout. Would you have given him a chance in your IT department? More information about hiring is included in chapter 4.

"A large employee population are type A, white-passing, 20–40 something females. Hiring outside of this persona would add variety. I fit this description and recognize that I benefit by being the dominant culture. I'm willing to give up my privilege for the sake of a richer community."

If hiring people for full-time positions isn't feasible, hiring consultants and subcontractors as well as vendors and suppliers can be an effective way to incorporate more diversity within a small business.

Small businesses may have smaller budgets to dedicate to DEI efforts, but this is not the place to cut corners. And it's never appropriate to take one or two marginalized employees and ask them to educate others in your company. If you're a white woman and someone asked you "How do white women feel about that?" you may respond, "I don't know. I'm only one person." Consider the Black man, lesbian or person who is an Arapaho tribal member. Can that person speak for the entire group? They may have anecdotal information—but anecdotes and stories are not the same thing as quantitative and qualitative data.

Qualitative Example

"As a Jewish person coming into leadership, I was clear there was no one like me on the team. In fact, when I did my orientation, I was struck by the consistently white, Irish or English descent, Christian or Catholic women that I met again and again. Similarly, I was disappointed not to see Black American, Asian American or Latinx colleagues on the leadership team and only 2 Africans on that team when I arrived (now 3)."

—Anonymous

Quantitative Example

With which race/ethnicity do you identify? Check all that apply.							
American Indian or Alaska Native							<5
Asian or Asian American							<5
Black or African American							<5
Hawaiian or Other Pacific Islander							<5
Hispanic or Latino							<5
White or Caucasian	9.4%	31.54%	38.93%	16.11%	4.03%	3.3%	149
Other/Multiracial							<5

Note that if there are fewer than five in a demographic group, the results to the question are not shown to protect anonymity. This means that in this organization, fewer than five people in any racial/ethnic demographic other than white were represented in this assessment's results.

In the above data example, there are more than 149 respondents who answered a question in the Likert scale. The Likert scale is a rating system used in questionnaires that is designed to measure people's attitudes, opinions or perceptions. In this survey, there are not five or more in any of the racial/ethnic categories other than white or Caucasian. This quantitative data shows the organization is not ethnically or racially diverse.

Color within the Lines

When selecting a measurement tool, there are certain "should" and "should not" guidelines for question construction.

Questions/Statements Should

- mean the same thing to all respondents (i.e., use clear language, avoid colloquialisms or slang, consider English as a second language [ESL] respondents).

- evoke the truth (i.e., the deeper meaning you are seeking to uncover).

- be written at an eighth-grade reading level to include all employee levels and ESL employees.

- address only one topic per question or statement.

- accommodate all possible answers (i.e., each respondent should be able to comfortably select a response from the choices presented).

- follow comfortably from the previous question.

Real Examples

"Management shows that diversity is important through their actions."

Succinct. Clear. One dimension measured. We like this one a lot.

"I understand what diversity and inclusion means at our organization."

Clear and succinct. Notice it is specifically asking what it means "at our organization" and not diversity and inclusion in the world or in popular culture.

Questions/Statements Should Not

- have mutually exclusive options (i.e., contain two concepts that cancel each other out).

- imply a desired answer (i.e., no leading the witness, Your Honor).

- use emotionally loaded or vaguely defined words (e.g., *trigger event*).

- use unfamiliar words or abbreviations (i.e., please don't say *synergy*).

- ask for a rating of 1–5 because simple numbers may not be clear enough (e.g., does 1 mean "never" and 5 mean "always"?

Or the other way around? And does 3 mean "I don't understand the question"?).

- depend on responses to previous questions (i.e., you should be able to randomize the order of the questions).

Real Examples

"Our organization's diversity/multicultural board committee meets consistently, has established meeting objectives and regularly provides progress reports to the board of directors and/or senior management."

Too many variables in this one. One variable per question.

"Our organization is happy that it has an accurate and up-to-date awareness of the diversity profile of our beneficiaries and stakeholders."

Can an organization be happy? How does one know this? How is it measured?

"The profile of our employees appropriately reflects the diversity of our beneficiaries and stakeholders."

Once again, unclear. What does "profile" mean (e.g., age, gender, race, abilities, income level)? What does "appropriately" mean? Are the beneficiaries and stakeholders the same people?

A self-assessment report may raise the consciousness of the individual taking the survey and increase awareness, thereby improving behavior by some small amount. More importantly, a DEI survey can provide action steps for an individual or an organization or both.

. . . .

"The Executive Committee is prioritizing DEI work now but is
entirely white, so it lacks the perspective of lived experience.
Ideally there would be more POC (People of Color) with a
seat at the table. Also, the Executive Committee should ask
BIPOC (Black, Indigenous and People of Color) what they
need rather than making the decisions for them."

—Anonymous

. . . .

A diversity, equity and inclusion self-assessment survey can

- reveal an organization's perceived commitment to diversity, equity and inclusion;

- indicate action items that those heading the effort internally would like to address because of the organization's results;

- determine individual development opportunities to focus training efforts based on the findings; and

- help individuals by increasing awareness of their personal cultural lens and how that lens impacts others around diversity, equity and inclusion issues.

Exceptions to the Rule

Research tells us that there are some demographics that do not display results that are consistent with the norm, meaning that their results are not as accurate as the results of others. One example group is physicians. The evidence suggests that physicians have a limited ability to accurately self-assess. The processes currently used to undertake professional development and evaluate competence among physicians may need to focus more on external assessment. Why? Because with physicians there was a low correlation between the self-evaluation and observations from others.

People may have an anecdote about a particularly sensitive—or insensitive—physician; however, the data tells the real story. This is a version of the Dunning-Kruger effect, which can occur when people who excel in a certain area think that the task is simple for everyone when it's not. The Dunning-Kruger effect can also happen when people who lack certain skills or abilities are seemingly oblivious to that fact and they consequently overestimate their own competence.

DUNNING KRUGER EFFECT

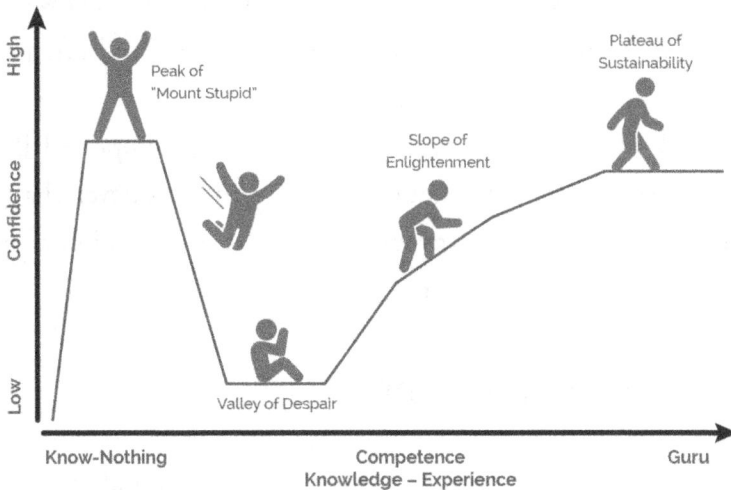

The physician research correlates with the Spectra Diversity data showing that CEOs, C-suite executives and SVPs often rate their organization higher than the other employees rate the organization's management, culture and three Ps (policies, practices and procedures). Spectra Diversity clients have speculated that the reason the upper-level executives rank these three categories higher is because they have more information at their fingertips. This is not something that the data can tell us.

The data tells us the "what" and cannot tell us the "why."

How to Measure?

When an organization decides to measure their diversity, equity and inclusion behaviors, they are often at a loss regarding what to do next. Many organizations are at the beginning of their DEI journey. Their organization follows basic federally mandated antidiscrimination laws to avoid negative consequences. They focus on treating everyone the same way—which we've learned is not what people want. People want to be treated the way *they* want to be treated, not how *you* want to treat them. Many organizations tend to be reactive and often stop initiatives once they are in legal compliance.

Think of all the organizations that said they supported Black Lives Matter during the summer of 2020 and then never changed hiring policies or shifted in any meaningful way to dismantle systemic racism existing within their organization.

Seven Measurement Tips

1. Don't wait to measure. Do it now. Those in underrepresented groups are feeling their power. Power is shifting from employer power to employee power. Small- and medium-size businesses are competing against the Fortune 500, 100 and 50 companies.

2. Select a measurement tool that has been statistically validated. If you ask an assessment organization for their

"psychometric report" and they say "Huh?" or "We have one from twenty years ago"—then move on. A statistically validated survey is highly valuable in terms of reliable insights and accurate data.

3. DEI challenges are markedly consistent among organizations. If your organization is facing lack of budget, difficulty working across functional areas and a lack of accepted DEI benchmarks, you're not alone. This is another reason for you to measure now.

4. Measurement is key to successful DEI strategy. More than half of all organizations have been attempting to do something DEI related for at least four years. One of the areas that has been tracked consistently by human resources departments is workforce demographics. This tells an organization about diversity but does nothing to measure inclusion.

5. Effective organizations track more, measure more and reward more. Advanced organizations have successfully used DEI metrics to make the business case for culture change.

6. Align your DEI goals with your organization's strategic goals and values.

7. Capture both qualitative data (comments and stories) and quantitative data (numbers and facts).

Knowing where the organization's commitment lies on the diversity, equity and inclusion continuum matters greatly. An organization that recognizes how DEI directly affects employee engagement and innovation is a forward-thinking, inclusive organization. When employees believe their organization is invested in diversity and inclusion efforts and that all stakeholders (employees, customers, partners) feel welcomed, valued, respected and heard, the result is a more engaged workforce. Organizations benefit by seeing an increase in productivity, innovation and morale.

Measurement is key. It's never too late to start.

Once you establish your DEI baseline, the real work comes in knowing what to do with that information. We begin to explore that process in chapter 3.

LEARNING ACTIVITY

How Much Do You Know? (Answers in Appendix)

Adding "salary negotiable" to job postings successfully reduced the gender gap in applications by _____ percent.

50

Research shows that the best way to remedy the effect of our implicit bias is to _____ with a diverse group of people and experience situations that may put us outside our comfort zone.

53

In 2015, Hispanic people had $1.5 trillion in buying power, a staggering _____ percent increase from 2010.

immerse ourselves in opportunities to make positive connections

Companies ranking in the top quartile of executive-board diversity had return on equity (ROE) _____ percent higher, on average, than companies in the bottom quartile.

generate consistently better ideas

A University of Chicago empirical study indicated that people with more diverse sources of information _____.

45

ACTION ITEMS

❏ Measure now. We've said this before because it's really, really important.

❏ Select a statistically validated measurement tool using a Likert scale so you get reliable, actionable data.

❏ Capture quantitative as well as qualitative data.

❏ Measure both the individual and the organization if you can. Each can benefit from the insights provided by the report.

CHAPTER 3

How Can You Drive Change in Your Organization?

Progress is impossible without change, and those who cannot change their minds cannot change anything.

—GEORGE BERNARD SHAW

How Diverse Is Your Universe? Change Begins with You

If you hold a senior leadership position in the United States, chances are you're a white male. That's just the way it is right now.

In 2020 almost 90 percent of the Fortune 500 CEOs were still white males. Is the same true for the leadership in your organization? What about your board of directors?

If you are going to power your organization's inclusive culture, the change must begin with you.

Diversity and inclusion are the tools you'll need to progress. Equity and belonging are the results.

Jim Rohn was a businessman, a self-made millionaire before he turned thirty-one, author, motivational speaker and even Anthony Robbins's mentor. He said, "You must take personal responsibility. You cannot change the circumstances, the seasons or the wind, but you can change yourself. That is something you have charge of."

Harvard Business Review reported that

1. 5.3 percent of large US companies have **CEOs named John**, compared to

2. 4.5 percent of organizations that have a **CEO named David**, compared to

3. **4.1 percent of organizations that have CEOs who are women.**

LEARNING ACTIVITY

How diverse is the world in which you operate? Here's a short exercise.

PEOPLE YOU TRUST	AGE	GENDER	SEXUAL ORIENTATION	RACE/ ETHNICITY	ABILITY STATUS

Make a list of the ten people you trust most—not including family. Don't worry if you don't have ten.

In the "People You Trust" row, write down at the top of the columns your age, gender, sexual orientation, race/ethnicity and ability status.

Done?

Now make a check mark next to everyone on your trust list who is *not* like you in terms of age, gender, sexual orientation, race/ethnicity and ability.

If you're like most people, the people you trust mirror your own demographics. You may have only one or two check marks on your page. At Spectra Diversity, our diversity and inclusion facilitators have done this activity, and another like it, many times. It is a truism that we generally like and trust people who are like us. It's called an *affinity bias*—a term used to describe how we subconsciously gravitate toward people who we feel share our interests, beliefs and background.

Overcoming Affinity Bias

There are no foreign lands. It is the traveler only who is foreign.

—ROBERT LOUIS STEVENSON

One of the ways in which we can overcome our affinity bias is by becoming familiar with the unfamiliar.

In 1979 I was part of the opening crew of a restaurant. Most of us were "in-between" workers who had graduated from college and not yet launched into our careers. Two of the men working there became my good friends and later became a couple. We vacationed together for decades and met socially many times during many years. They introduced me to their gay friends—many of whom died in the first wave of the AIDS epidemic.

Enter my dad—a retired civil engineer who is conservative, religious and a World War II vet. Gay men did not figure into his life growing up. At parties, holidays and other gatherings, my dad came to know my two gay friends. Over time, they came to like each other. We all went to my parents' cabin. We played bridge. We laughed at "dad jokes." Recently, during COVID-19 when everyone was house bound, my ninety-four-year-old dad asked how the couple was doing. "I really miss those guys." Dad overcame his affinity bias against gay men by getting to know my good friends.

It's my belief that affinity bias can be undone to a certain extent by meeting and interacting with people who are not like you. By interacting, I'm not referring to saying hello in the grocery checkout line. I'm referring to doing something together—a book club, a dinner invitation, a regular time to walk together. Interacting needs more than just proximity.

Types of Bias

We've only discussed three biases so far—here are some of the more than 150 that can affect an organization:

- **Affinity Bias**—Having the tendency to prefer or seek out those like oneself.

- **Anchoring Bias**—Having the tendency to rely heavily upon the first piece of information available rather than seeking out and fully evaluating multiple sources of information when making a decision.

- **Belief Bias**—Having the tendency to decide whether an argument for something is strong or weak based upon whether one agrees with the conclusion of that argument.

- **Blind Spot**—Identifying biases in others but not oneself.

- **Confirmation Bias**—Having the tendency to seek information that confirms preexisting beliefs or assumptions, or conversely to discount information that is incongruent with one's assumptions.

- **Correspondence Bias**—The tendency to draw inferences about a person's unique and enduring dispositions from behaviors that can be entirely explained by the situations in which they occur.

- **Groupthink**—Having the tendency to try and fit into a group by either mimicking their behavior or holding back on sharing thoughts and opinions out of fear of potential exclusion.

- **Halo Effect**—Having the tendency to believe only good about someone because they are liked or letting someone's positive qualities in one area influence the overall perception of that person.

- **In-Group Bias**—Perceiving those who are similar in a more positive way.

- **Out-Group Bias**—Perceiving those who are different in a more negative way.

- **Perception Bias**—Having the tendency to form assumptions or stereotypes about certain groups—thus making it impossible to make objective decisions about members of those groups.

The implicit-association test, or unconscious bias test, is one of twelve implicit-association tests that you can take at this link: https://implicit.harvard.edu/implicit/takeatest.html

They're free. They're confidential. They are guaranteed to be enlightening.

When you start the process of building respect and increasing your emotional intelligence and resilience, you may feel uncomfortable. To make progress in diversity, equity and inclusion, you'll need to become comfortable with feeling uncomfortable.

Be the Change

Change can happen from both the top down and the bottom up. A good way to start when you're at the top is to lead by example. There are small actions you can take to act as a role model. One example is to add your pronouns to your email signature, Zoom signature and website bio page. This is not something to mandate, however. Imagine how it would feel to be the only "they" in a sea of "he/him" and "she/her" name badges. It would be akin to being the only one to show up at a black-tie dinner wearing a sport coat.

When considering the DEI continuum, each individual will fall somewhere on the Maturity Model shown below.

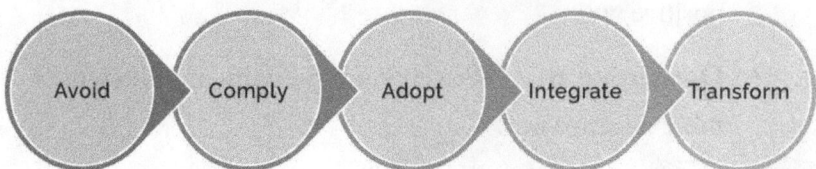

Avoid → Comply → Adopt → Integrate → Transform

As one might expect, there are few individuals and organizations at the end of this spectrum, with most clustered in the middle three sections. The actions and beliefs of the five stages include, but are not limited to, the following:

- **Avoid:** Little or no awareness of diversity and inclusion. Cultural differences are generally thought of as food, clothing and celebrations. Behaviors may include shaming and blaming others, initiating humor at the expense of others, holding beliefs that others are inferior or should be avoided, demonstrating lack of trust and avoiding or withdrawing from cultural differences.

- **Comply:** Goes along to get along. Pays lip service to diversity and inclusion in the workplace. Behaviors may include tolerating humor at the expense of others, remaining quiet or uninvolved when witnessing microaggressions, lacking knowledge about those who are different from self and viewing cultural differences in terms of "us versus them."

- **Adopt:** Works to include others, acknowledges and respects differences, understands that we are the way we are because of our cultural backgrounds and influences, recognizes and appreciates patterns related to culture, ethnicity, gender, age and other dimensions of diversity.

- **Integrate:** Able to interact with different people, able to perform tasks with comfort and ease in interactions with those who are different from "self." Models and promotes appropriate inclusive behaviors.

- **Transform:** A visionary; actively incorporates inclusionary behavior in interactions. Holds themselves accountable for creating and sustaining a diverse and inclusive culture.

Most individuals are somewhere in the adopt phase. To be a more inclusive individual, and a more transformative leader, you need to begin by working on yourself.

Become Comfortable with Being Uncomfortable

If you're a white cisgender male, you may be feeling vulnerable at this point. That's understandable. As a white cisgender female, I've had to learn a lot about how women of color have had to navigate the world differently than I have. It can feel strange to look back on your entire life and wonder how it may have been different if you were disabled in some manner, were in the LGBTQ community or were BIPOC rather than white. It doesn't mean that you didn't work hard to get to where you are. It means that you started at the starting line, and someone else may have started back fifty yards. We'll cover this in more depth in chapter 5 on race.

If you're just beginning to connect with those in your out-group, you should probably expect to be uncomfortable. Any new skill that is being developed feels a little awkward at first. When you feel uncomfortable, accept it.

I had a personal lesson in this when I joined a book club that was primarily Black and brown women. We met through Zoom. I learned very quickly that there was lingo that I didn't know. Once something was described as very "bougie." I waited a bit, then later I said, "Can we go back to that word? What's 'bougie'?" They all chuckled—in a nice way. It turns out it was short for *bourgeoisie*—which I did know! I also didn't know about *CPT*—"Colored People Time." And I learned that my book club friends can use the phrase, but it would be disrespectful of me to use it. To top it off, I didn't know some of the Black historical figures that they all knew. I had to learn to be an attentive listener when they spoke about common issues they had all faced (such as strangers touching their hair) that I had not.

The moral of this story is that little by little, the brain, my brain, has been rewired. I listen with curiosity. I don't expect my fellow book clubbers to act as Google for me. I apologize if I inadvertently step on someone's toes. I'm comfortable being uncomfortable.

Remind yourself that everyone is on a different part of the DEI journey. It's a process—not a destination. So celebrate the travel!

Everyone you will ever meet knows something you don't.

—BILL NYE

Are You an Inclusive Leader?

How can you tell if your company is heading in the direction of inclusion? How do you know if you have been an inclusive leader? We already learned that inclusion is a necessary ingredient in the DEI mix. Being a leader requires many skills, one of which is learning how to be inclusive and promote change within an organization that may be reluctant to change.

. . . .

"Previously (before the current Executive Director) I was not considered for employment or a role in leadership. I believe this was based on my ethnicity. Since we have had a new ED, I have been given a fair look and feel more valued."

—Anonymous

. . . .

Betsy Bagley, cofounder and client success director of Pulsely, maintains that while many DEI initiatives begin at a grassroots level among employees (looking at you, Starbucks), organizational impact is often elusive until senior leaders become engaged.

Have you had good employees leave your organization? More importantly, have you had good employees who were in a marginalized or underrepresented group leave your organization because they didn't feel as though they belonged? What do your exit interviews tell you? Has HR or a people manager told you that an employee who left "wasn't a good fit"? If you hear they weren't a good fit, your ears should perk up. People from all walks of life can be a good fit if your culture is diverse and inclusive.

In contrast, a toxic corporate culture is the strongest predictor of industry-adjusted attrition. According to a recent study, a toxic culture is ten times more important than compensation in predicting turnover. The analysis found that the leading elements contributing to toxic cultures include failure to promote diversity, equity and inclusion; workers feeling disrespected; and unethical behavior.

Consider this:

- Groups formerly seen as minorities may reach majority status by 2044.

- Forty-eight percent of Generation Z are racial or ethnic minorities.

- Diverse companies enjoy 2.5 times higher cash flow per employee.

- Diverse management increases revenue by 19 percent.

- Gender-diverse companies are 15 percent more likely to beat industry median financial returns.

- More than three out of four workers prefer diverse companies.

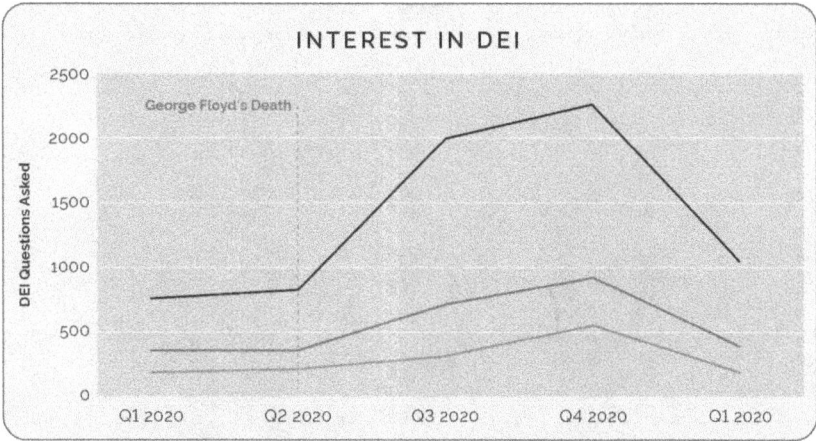

INTEREST IN DEI

Spectra Diversity's qualitative data supports the above graphic and proves the point that organizational support for Black Lives Matter may have been performative only.

I receive boots-on-the-ground information from Spectra Diversity's Change Partners. Our Spectra Partners directly serve organizations which use the Spectra Assessment to measure their clients' organizations and the individuals within those organizations. They're all seeing the falloff of interest in DEI work.

The interest is waning—though the importance is not.

Leaders: Do You Have What It Takes?

You may be wondering if you have the qualities and skills that support being an inclusive CEO or leader. Spectra Diversity data tells us that leaders typically view their organization through rose-colored glasses. Let's assume that's not you!

To become a more inclusive individual and a more transformative leader, you need to begin by working on yourself. Three key aspects of being an inclusive leader are

- resilience,
- emotional intelligence and
- respect.

Resilience

Resilience is not a short-term concept. It is a long-term perspective that is particularly revealing during turbulent times such as the COVID-19 pandemic. A resilient leader is an optimistic thinker who understands reality and works to find the positive aspects of adversity while putting focus on future opportunities. A resilient leader has personal values that are shown and present in the workplace. Resilient leaders have confidence and the competence to be consistent when faced with challenges. Resilient leaders have a strong support base and maintain a focus on their personal well-being. Resilient leaders persevere; they are adaptable. They are courageous decision-makers, and they take personal responsibility for their actions.

As this draft was being edited, another mass shooting occurred in Highland Park, Illinois, during a Fourth of July parade. The mayor of the town is an example of resilience. Mayor Nancy Rotering used a mayor's handbook for mass shootings (yes, there is such a thing) and immediately put herself out front and center for interviews and actions to support the families who were affected by either death, wounding or witnessing. She showed confidence in a time of extreme challenge and put a focus on the well-being of her citizens.

Prior to forming Spectra Diversity, I was involved in creating a resilience assessment profile for Human Perspectives International

(HPI). It provides individual and group analysis in eleven areas of thinking skills, capacity skills and action skills. Accurate measurement is always valued, and the HPI assessment, based on years of data collected by the authors, can help determine your resilience readiness.

Emotional Intelligence

Daniel Goleman defines emotional intelligence as "the capacity for recognizing our own feelings and those of others, for motivating ourselves and for managing emotions well in ourselves and our relationships." Research demonstrates that without awareness of one's own feelings and what is behind them, a person has virtually no chance of demonstrating self-regulation—the ability to manage one's feelings so that behaviors are appropriate for the situation.

Whether you are in manufacturing, finance, retail or government, as a leader or an employee you can benefit from emotional intelligence. Consider this: Coca-Cola trained its leaders in emotional intelligence and found that these individuals exceeded their performance targets by 15 percent, while, in contrast, leaders who did not develop emotional capabilities missed their targets by the same margin. That is a **30 percent gap**.

Putting Respect into Action

Neuroscience has shown that people can identify another person's main identity markers (race, gender, age, etc.) in a matter of milliseconds. In the blink of an eye, our primitive brain (the amygdala) has decided whether the other person is from our in-group (like us) or is from an out-group (unlike us).

The good news is that our brain has neuroplasticity—meaning it can be rewired for better outcomes. Over time, we can selectively rewire our brains with curiosity rather than stereotypes. And that curiosity leads to trust and respect. Organizations at all levels benefit from mutual respect. In Bantu (a language found in parts of Africa) the "process of developing mutual respect" is known as *ubuntu* (ooh-BUN-too). One of my colleagues, Lenora Billings-Harris, named her diversity and inclusion consulting business UbuntuGlobal.

"On one of my many trips to South Africa, I learned the meaning of ubuntu. One of the translations is: I am because we are. We are because I am. This view of the world embodies the true meaning of inclusion and diversity, in my view. We are all connected. What you do impacts me and vice versa. The more we understand ubuntu, my hope is the more likely as humans we will realize we need each other and can appreciate our differences and similarities."

— Lenora Billings-Harris

This is like the East Indian word *namaste* (nah-mah-STAY), which means "the spirit in me respects the spirit in you."

Paul Meshanko, in his book *The Respect Effect*, quotes Dr. Ellen Weber, director of the MITA International Brain Center: "Social fairness and respect help employees learn. When we show interest in others, support them and praise them genuinely, we release a chemical mix of serotonin and oxytocin into their brains. These neurotransmitters encourage trust, open others' minds to our ideas and creative desire to get to know us better and to help with whatever we need done."

How to Build Trust? Respect

Paul Meshanko recommends several rules of respect.

1. Be aware of your verbal and nonverbal cues and the way they can be interpreted. "Let's circle back to this" can mean "This is permanently on the back burner." "Interesting" can mean "I hate that idea." Arms folded can mean "I'm cold," "I'm hostile to your idea" or "I'm feeling a need to self-soothe or protect myself."

2. Develop curiosity about the perspectives of others. Try to make a habit of wondering why other people do or say things. If someone reacts in an extreme manner to a situation, explore it further. Ask yourself, "I wonder what made her respond that way?" If decisions are made without someone in the room whom it may affect, try to think, "I wonder how they might feel about that?"

3. Assume that everyone is smart about something. Albert Einstein said, "Everyone is a genius. But if you judge a fish on its ability to climb a tree, it will live its whole life feeling stupid." A standard phrase I use is "I don't know anything about that. Tell me more." If you believe that everyone can teach you something, you're on the road to becoming a lifelong learner. For example, just a few weeks ago, I discovered that jumper cables from one car to another car are no longer needed. The tow truck sent by AAA has remote battery chargers. Who knew? Not me.

4. Become a better listener by losing your "but." When speaking with someone, the words you use before saying *but* are immediately forgotten. "I really liked your presentation, but it could have been shorter and more to the point." Try instead the technique used in improv. When

someone says something that you may object to or have a different opinion of—substitute *and* for *but*.

Them: "I noticed we only have two women and no People of Color on our board of directors."

You: "Yes, that's true, *and* we're committed to increasing our board size and adding more racial and ethnic diversity."

5. When you disagree, explain why. You don't want to be the parent who says, "Because I said so." Explain your reasons—many of which the other person may be unaware of. Share the truth as you know it. Of course, this should go both ways. Each party should explain the *why* behind their *what*.

6. Learn to be wrong. If you've dug in your heels on an issue, it becomes harder and harder to relinquish your position, even in the face of overwhelming and contradictory evidence. Consider those in the Flat Earth Society. Mutual respect is difficult when one side is entrenched. When your idea or concept is challenged, ask yourself whether your earth is flat—or a globe? Are you dug in without a good reason or facts to support your position?

7. Don't hesitate to apologize. The key to this is that the apology must be authentic. "I'm sorry. Happy now?" would not be a welcome response. Nobody is perfect. If you've made an unintentionally disrespectful comment or behavior, say you're sorry—in public if it was a public statement or action, and in private if not. People are not good at remembering the details of a slight—and they are very good at remembering how the slight made them feel.

Don't wait to apologize. Do it as soon as you realize that you've made a mistake. Here's how:

"I apologize for _____."

"In the future I will _____."

8. Intentionally engage others in ways that build their self-esteem. It shows respect when you publicly acknowledge someone's contribution. If you're not a people person by nature, try to fake it until you make it. Those with whom you're engaging will appreciate the effort and can respect you for it.

Know When to Go with Your Gut

When we're listening to our gut or following a gut reaction, we're typically following our autopilot system. The average person spends about 47 percent of their day on autopilot, following automated behaviors while their thoughts wander from the task at hand. Equally intriguing, when the participants reported their mind wandering, they also reported being significantly less happy in that moment.

As the brain of our species developed, a very useful activity took place in the amygdala (which is nicknamed the "lizard brain"). This area of the brain helped our ancestors run away from life-threatening situations such as an encounter with saber-toothed cats. This is the part of the brain responsible for the fight, flight or freeze responses. This is our gut instinct. Rational thinking lies in the cognitive part of our brain, which is the prefrontal cortex. This is the rational-thinking and intentional-system portion of our brain.

Here's an example of when your gut feeling can be wrong:

Imagine you're minding your own business, driving, on your way to work. Suddenly someone pulls up behind you quickly—toots their horn repeatedly (when you're going the speed limit, thank you very much) and then zooms around you, almost cutting you off as they change lanes. Your gut says, "What a jerk!"

Now imagine your pregnant wife's water just broke—but in addition to the water, there seems to be a great deal of blood. You're rushing to the hospital, and someone won't pull over even though you honked at them to move over. You're worried about your wife, and her life is at stake. You're forced to pull around the obstinate driver to get to the hospital. Your gut says, "What a jerk!"

In each case you've attributed your thinking to the other driver. The scientific name for this error in thinking and feeling is the *correspondence bias*. The correspondence bias is the tendency to draw inferences about a person's unique and enduring dispositions from behaviors that can be entirely explained by the situations in which they occur.

Just because you are right, does not mean I am wrong.
You just haven't seen life from my side.

Should you go with your gut in professional interactions? Usually not.

For example, research shows that job interviews are a poor indicator of future job performance. The person you like in an interview is most likely a person like yourself in a variety of ways. Your gut will automatically separate interview subjects into an in-group and an out-group. Your autopilot system may lead you to be overconfident in your ability to judge people (overconfidence bias) and go with your gut on new hires when a more cognitive approach would yield optimal results. You could often benefit from hiring someone who is not like you at all and who has skills, attributes and a background unlike your own.

. . . .

"I believe that we need to look at firm, specific issues with respect to employing and promoting staff from diverse backgrounds—approaches to hiring, promotion, benefits, etc. I have heard little to nothing about this over the last year. Rather, I see a lot of time being spent on public statements, committees, book clubs, venues for airing feelings and other such activities. I have been told to say 'Black Lives Matter' by people who I don't think have any understanding of how adopting the BLM platform might align to, fail to align to or impact our organizational scope of work. Time would be better spent considering and adapting real, specific policies."

—Anonymous

. . . .

MIT recommends four actions you can take today to reduce attrition.

1. Provide opportunities for lateral job moves (keep your existing employees).

2. Sponsor corporate social events (fosters team building).

3. Offer remote-work options (the home office is here to stay).

4. Make schedules more predictable for frontline employees (show respect for blue-collar workers).

Start with Quick Wins

Just like the bow of a ship, the leader points the company in the direction it will go. You can be the tugboat that helps turn the ship around. Assuming you have measured your employees and collected both quantitative and qualitative data, there are going to be actions to take that are significant and long term. For example, increasing your managers' ability to act in an inclusive manner and create trust and a sense of belonging is not a quick fix. It will require training and ongoing reinforcement at a minimum, and coaching and new key performance indicators (KPIs) at the other end of the scale. For this reason, start with high-return, low-risk items (quick wins) to demonstrate to your employees that they were heard and that you're prepared to take action.

Comp Time Example

One organization that used the Spectra Assessment had a ton of comments about compensatory (comp) time—how it was used, when you could get it, the requirements and limitations. Employees were in an uproar about comp time! This was something that the leadership could fix relatively quickly. Examine the complaints. Outline the options to address the complaints. Change the policy. This could take just one month to implement—rather than one year for more difficult issues. It was a huge source of friction that those at the top could address relatively quickly.

Clarity Example

Another organization's employees didn't know who oversaw their diversity, equity and inclusion initiatives. Was it HR? Was it the chief operating officer? Their direct supervisor? If they had an issue, where should they take it? If the initial response was unsatisfactory, who was next in the chain of command? Basically, they had a communication issue. The leaders knew who was in charge—and the employees did not.

Holiday Example

Christians in the US get their holidays off—Christmas Eve, Christmas Day, Easter and occasionally others, such as Good Friday. Imagine you're Jewish, Muslim or Hindu. You're forced to *not* work and *not* get paid for a holiday you don't celebrate, and you must take a sick day or personal time off to celebrate your own religious holidays. This can be a bit trickier, but it's not unheard of for those who practice non-Christian religions to have paid time off for their religious holidays. Or perhaps all employees are given a certain number of floating days off that are separate from sick days. Those floating days could be used for other purposes too—such as going to vote on Election Day or caring for a relative who is ill.

"One time our CEO's newsletter said, 'This time of year would mean nothing if it wasn't for our savior Jesus Christ.' I voiced concerns that such a statement may not be received well by staff and thought that I had a safe space to share the feedback as a way to help our organization be more inclusive. Instead, I was instructed to not challenge our approach and that nothing would change."

—Anonymous

ERG Example

Create ERGs (employee resource groups) in your organization. An ERG leader can play several roles. AVTAR, based in India, outlines these roles for ERG leaders:

- Achiever—accomplishes integrated business goals with the ERG
- Champion—defends equal opportunity for all
- Catalyst—advocates for policy restructuring and actioning
- Benefactor—sponsors events for community development
- Inspirer—volunteers to work at the grassroots level
- Ally—supports with no judgment of identity or interests
- Influencer—inspires future leaders through encouragement and motivation

It's important for ERGs to have a stated mission and vision for the group and for the organization to provide some funding. It's also important to allow anyone to join any ERG. A white cisgender male who is curious about the Black employee experience could join the BIPOC ERG in any of the above roles.

A-B-C-D-E: Five Simple Actions

We now know that diversity and inclusion are the tools to achieve equity and belonging. And we know that change must happen at the top. If you're at the top, you start by working on yourself in terms of resilience, emotional intelligence and respect. Then what do you do?

On an organizational level, you can measure how your employees view management; culture; and your policies, practices and procedures. That will give you organizational data. To help you work on your own behaviors, Spectra Diversity teaches individuals to practice five simple actions.

The five simple actions below are the keys to modifying your belief system and developing interpersonal skills that foster inclusion.

1. **Acknowledge unconscious bias.** We all have it. Reflect on your behavior when you have a gut reaction, and use storytelling to bridge the gap between yourself and anyone who is unlike you in some significant demographic or other way.

2. **Be present, and pause.** This can also refer to sidelining your gut reaction by taking a moment to pause and let your cognitive brain come to the forefront. A pause offers opportunity to make a different and better or more inclusive choice. It sidelines the lizard brain.

3. **Consider the other person's point of view.** We do this by listening without judgment and checking our assumptions. Assume good intent. Mindfulness is an excellent activity

that can help you provide an opportunity to consider the other person's point of view.

4. **Determine what to do differently.** Your actions and your words can result in a person feeling either marginalized or as though they matter. There is a positive-feedback-sandwich trick I learned many years ago, in which the two pieces of bread are positive comments and the flavor between the bread slices is either a corrective comment or a clarifying question. It looks like this: positive statement—clarifying statement or question—positive statement.

5. **Engage others through dialogue.** You've learned that most people do not have a diverse universe. You can start taking baby steps to broaden that universe. Take the family out to an ethnic restaurant. Visit a place of worship that is not of your religion. Ask a colleague (who is not like you) to lunch or dinner. When you meet people and talk to them (like in the story with my dad and my friends), you may find you have much more in common than any visible differences.

Hire diversity. Follow with inclusion. Turn your ship around!

LEARNING ACTIVITY

How Much Do You Know? (Answers in Appendix)

_____ percent of leaders agreed that the D&I agenda is a top priority, but only 34 percent believed that it's a strength in their workplace. In another survey, 80 percent of HR professionals viewed companies as "going through the motions."

99

In 2018, fifty-one companies in the S&P 500 included a diversity metric in their compensation program. By February 2021, that number had increased to _____ companies.

93

Companies that disclose EEO-1 reports outperformed their Russell 1000 peers in the stock market by _____ percent in 2021.

73

_____ percent of Americans want companies to publicize the ethnic and racial makeup of their organization.

2.4

___ percent of CEOs see that the lack of trust in their organization lies in their diversity, equity and inclusion practices.

41

ACTION ITEMS

❏ Start at the top. Work on increasing your emotional intelligence and resilience. You'll need these qualities to move your organization forward.

❏ Become comfortable with feeling uncomfortable. You can be a role model in this regard.

❏ Respect all people at all times. When you assume good intent and treat people with respect, it will increase employee engagement and productivity.

❏ Use your DEI assessment to determine the quick wins, and make those changes ASAP.

❏ Use your qualitative and quantitative data to develop a long-term DEI strategy that aligns with your organization's mission, vision and values.

CHAPTER 4

Do All Genders Feel Respected and Heard?

Women belong in all places where decisions are being made. It shouldn't be that women are the exception.

—RUTH BADER GINSBURG

What Is Gender, Anyway?

Ruth Bader Ginsberg was responsible for many rulings as an attorney arguing before the US Supreme Court. The American Civil Liberties Union (ACLU) reported that "often, she argued that men were being discriminated against. Ginsburg sometimes said that one of her favorite cases involved a man whose wife died in childbirth, leaving him alone to care for their newborn son. Stephen Wiesenfeld's wife had been the primary breadwinner, and upon her death, he went to the local Social Security office to inquire about survivors' benefits for a parent and learned that he didn't qualify because he was a man. Ginsburg convinced the Supreme Court that the section of the Social Security Act that denied fathers benefits because of their sex was unconstitutional. She won a unanimous decision."

By arguing that men were being discriminated against, she was able to give *power* to women, so men weren't necessary to *empower* the women.

To understand gender, we need to turn off our binary way of thinking. Our brains are wired to classify people into ones who belong in our in-group and ones who are in our out-group. The problem with this binary thinking is that gender is like the other demographics that make up diversity. It is not a yes/no or in/out classification. It's a continuum.

It's easy to start thinking of the LGBTQ community when you begin to think of gender in the workplace. However, only the *T* (for transgender) in *LGBTQ* belongs to the gender discussion. The other four letters belong to sexual orientation. Because the LGBTQ community shares the identity of being discriminated against, transgender people are often included with the others. Think of LGBTQ as an antidiscrimination social justice grouping. The *T* belongs under the gender category, and the lesbian, gay, bisexual and questioning or queer belong in sexual orientation.

Continuum of Gender

Gender in thousands

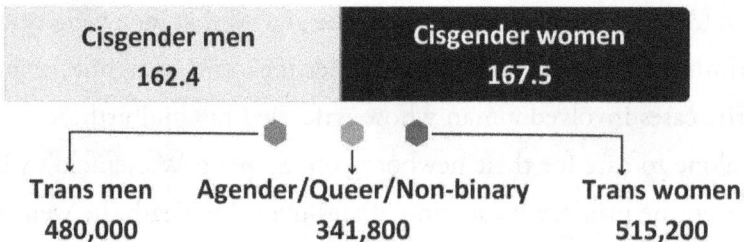

Cisgender men 162.4	Cisgender women 167.5

Trans men 480,000	Agender/Queer/Non-binary 341,800	Trans women 515,200

Gender has a range from cisgender men on one end to cisgender women on the other end. This continuum contains both the physical and the psychological aspects of gender.

- **Agender** means that a person identifies as not having a gender. A person who identifies within this term will often consider themselves either as having a type of nonbinary gender identity or as not subscribing to any gender identity at all.

- **Cisgender** is commonly used to refer to people who identify exclusively with the gender that they were assigned at birth. For example, a woman who was born with female organs and identifies as a woman is a cisgender woman.

- **Genderqueer** describes a gender identity that cannot be defined as exclusively masculine or feminine. Genderqueer people experience their gender in all unique ways (hence the name). The impossibility of defining the term is part of its appeal for people who identify as genderqueer. The identity can include elements of feminine, masculine or nonbinary identities or none of these. In part, it can be seen as a rejection of association with a label.

- **Nonbinary** is widely used to describe a gender identity that cannot be categorized as masculine or feminine. Nonbinary people experience their gender in all different ways. It could be experienced as a combination of male and female, neither male nor female or something completely independent of notions of conventional gender identities. Nonbinary is an expansive umbrella term, and many gender identities fall under it.

- **Transgender or trans** is used to describe any person who has a gender identity that is different from the gender that they were assigned at birth. For example: a transgender woman is a woman who was born a man and who identifies as a woman (with or without surgery or hormones).

When you look at the continuum of gender (ignoring sexual orientation), there are subtleties that typically do not show up in the data charts. Where would you place the following individuals?

- **Gender dysphoria**—According to the American Psychiatric Association, gender dysphoria is "a concept designated in the DSM-5 as clinically significant distress or impairment related to a strong desire to be of another gender, which may include desire to change primary and/or secondary sex characteristics. Not all transgender or gender diverse people experience dysphoria." So if a man or woman is masking their gender dysphoria, where would you place them on the gender continuum?

- **Intersex individuals**—According to Planned Parenthood, "intersex is a general term used for a variety of situations in which a person is born with reproductive or sexual anatomy that doesn't fit the boxes of 'female' or 'male.' Sometimes doctors do surgeries on intersex babies and children to make their bodies fit binary ideas of male or female. Doctors always assign intersex babies a legal sex (male or female, in most states), but just like with nonintersex people, it doesn't mean that's the gender identity they'll grow up to have. This brings up questions about whether it's OK to do medical procedures on children's bodies when it's not needed for their health."

- **Tomboy**—This is a girl who enjoys rough, noisy activities traditionally associated with boys. A woman can be a tomboy just during childhood or for her entire lifetime. If gender is a continuum, would you place tomboys toward the center of the line next to transgender women?

- **Two-Spirit People**—Native Americans have often held intersex, androgynous people, feminine males and masculine females in high respect. The most common term to define such persons today is to refer to them as "two-spirit" people.

Walter L. Williams, author of *The Spirit and the Flesh*, says that "since everything that exists is thought to come from the spirit world, androgynous or transgender persons are seen as doubly blessed, having both the spirit of a man and the spirit of a woman. Thus, they are honored for having two spirits and are seen as more spiritually gifted than the typical masculine male or feminine female."

- **XXY men**—There are men who have an extra X chromosome. Instead of XY, they have XXY. It's called Klinefelter's syndrome. These men don't typically show any signs of this condition until puberty. They usually have trouble fathering biological children because of a low sperm count. They have other conditions during adulthood which can benefit from treatment.

Men and Women at Work

Cisgender men and women account for 98–99 percent of the workforce, with the transgender and other gender population making up the other 1–2 percent. How do the genders stack up in the workplace?

Here's some data to consider:

- There are 1.4 million transgender individuals in the US (0.6 percent of US adults).

- The percentage of women in the workforce has been stagnant since the 1990s. Eighty-eight percent of men are in the workforce, compared to 76 percent of women.

- Women of color face double challenges. Forty percent of Black women have had their judgment questioned in their area of expertise, compared to 27 percent of men.

- Women earn less than men in nearly all occupations. For every dollar a man earns, women earn 82 cents for the same job. This wage gap increases over the lifetime of a career.

- In the US women are still underrepresented in leadership, with just 32.6 percent in management, according to Catalyst. Women who are BIPOC are even fewer.

  □ Latinas: 4.3 percent

  □ Black women: 4.3 percent

  □ Asian women: 2.7 percent

In our Spectra Diversity assessments, we found more women exist in certain fields such as healthcare, human resources and service industries. These women can make up most of the workforce—although they may not be included in like numbers within leadership positions.

Women are increasingly leaving the world of "employee" and joining the world of "employer."

- Women-owned firms made up only 19.9 percent of all firms that employed people in the United States in 2018, but their numbers are growing.

- There were 6,861 more women-owned firms in 2018 than in 2017, up 0.6 percent to 1.1 million.

- Women-owned employer firms reported nearly $1.8 trillion in sales, shipments, receipts or revenue and employed over 10.1 million workers with an annual payroll of $388.1 billion in 2018.

Look at the smart, productive, creative and hardworking women in your organization. How many of them are willing to leave your organization to form their own company?

Consider that being a woman does not mean that you have a uterus and can carry babies—many women don't and can't. Being a woman does not mean that you're feminine—many women aren't. It does not mean you were born in the right body. Caitlyn Jenner is now a woman. Chaz Bono and Elliot Page are now men. Gender is a continuum—not a black-and-white issue. If you, as a leader, have a growth mindset, you'll want to see the gray that lies between the black and white.

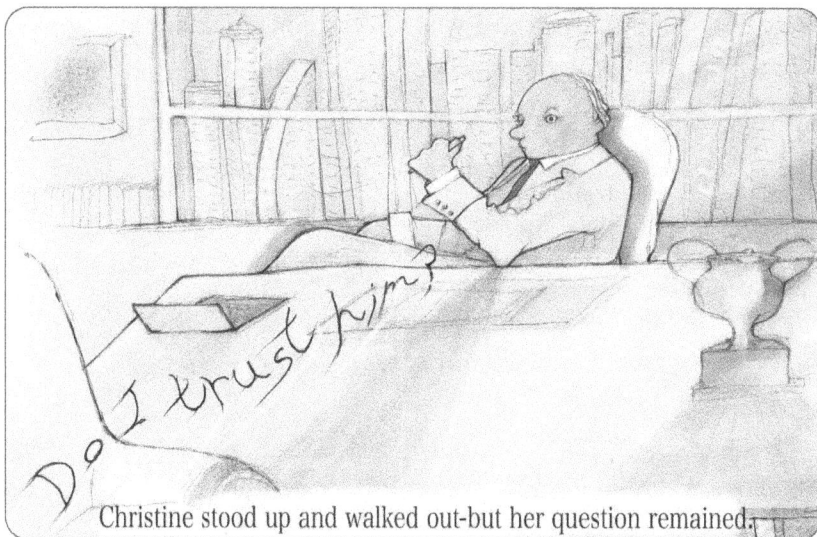

Christine stood up and walked out-but her question remained.

Seeing the Gray: What Is a Woman?

When I was growing up in the '50s and '60s, it was easy to tell who the woman was. She was the one in a dress or a skirt! I grew up in a time when the dress code at school prohibited pants. So little girls who wanted to swing on the jungle gym did so with their bare legs hanging out and underwear showing when the breeze blew. By the time I was in college, the women were in torn jeans and the men had long hair. You could still tell them apart by how they talked, what their interests were and the occasional facial hair. I thought I could also tell the genders apart.

How wrong I was. I learned about the term *gender dysphoria* in 2016. Remember that there are 1.4 million transgender people in the workforce. You may have a trans person in your organization and not know it unless they choose to reveal their identity to you.

I met Rebecca when Spectra Diversity hired Purrly Digital LLC as a front-end and back-end developer for the creation of our assessment and reporting. We met through a referral from a colleague. At that time, she was presenting as a male, was married and had two biological children. For those who haven't done it before, developing a new online product is a time-consuming process. There are decisions to make, questions to answer and computer bugs to smash. Purrly and Spectra worked well together and launched the Spectra Diversity Inclusion Assessment (SDIA) in 2017. We had a product, a rainbow-colored logo, a DEI Facilitation Kit for training and high hopes for the future. What we did not know, however, was the turmoil developing in the life of Purrly Digital's owner, Rebecca.

CASE STUDY: Rebecca

I had known since kindergarten that something was different. By second grade I knew what it was and in junior high found the language to describe it. Since that time, I have "come out" to friends and family five times prior to this last time in 2017. I had figured out [how] to hide being transgender and control the gender dysphoria (the distress a person feels because of their birth-assigned sex and gender not matching their gender identity) and basically just pretend.

Day to day life in 2017 was outwardly pretty normal. I was building a business and had been doing it full time for two years. I had employees. My kids were four and two. I was pretending, though. Dysphoria gets worse the older you get, and I was almost thirty-seven when I came out for the last time. In February of 2017, I told my wife, and she was blindsided. She had no idea. She was in Texas with a friend, and I had stayed home to work. It was at this time that I attempted to commit suicide. I went to Target, bought a bottle of pills and took them all. While I was waiting for the pills to work, I had second thoughts and ran to the bathroom to throw up as much as I could. Apparently, it was enough. I slept for eighteen hours afterward.

Not sharing feelings had become normal for me. Omission of details becomes ingrained. In retrospect, there was not a better client to come out to than Spectra Diversity.

My other clients were all great. I think it's a testament to how I ran the business. One was even a Trump supporter, and he's still a client. I had been using Rebecca as an alias name, and in 2018 I switched so that Rebecca was my online name. Your alias and online name are meaningful in the tech industry.

In February 2018 I came out socially on Facebook and mailed a letter to my extended family. I got a ton of blowback from my family—which hurt. My marriage was crumbling. Several of my clients, including Spectra Diversity, had to go away when I couldn't support them adequately. I also laid off my staff. During that time, I was also in therapy for a sexual assault that happened in fifth grade. [The year] 2018 was a disaster. My worst professional and personal year ever.

TRANSGENDER NAMING

To be legally recognized as who I am was a massive deal. The court date was July 24, 2018. I had letters from my psychologist, surgeon and endocrinologist. And I had people there who were willing to testify to my new identity. It was a really big event for me. The rest of 2018 was tough. My partner and I separated in October 2018. I was living off credit cards (thank goodness I had excellent credit) and depressed. I basically couldn't work full time for fifteen months.

Rebecca (center back row); Chris (second from right middle row)

94

In 2022, Spectra Diversity resumed working with Rebecca and her team at Purrly Digital. Rebecca shares custody of her two children and is living separately from her former spouse. At this point in time, I consider Rebecca a friend as well as a colleague. It's been a great privilege to be trusted with her story and to share in her journey.

So, once more, what is a woman?

In a recent Supreme Court confirmation hearing, Justice Ketanji Brown Jackson was asked by Senator Marsha Blackburn, R-Tenn., "Can you provide a definition for the word 'woman'?" Jackson responded, "I'm not a biologist."

"Equal rights for others does not mean less rights for you. There's not a limited supply of rights."

Women in the Workplace

Being a woman does mean certain things in our society and in the workplace. Here are some numbers regarding your average everyday woman in the workplace in 2022:

- More than half of women are more stressed than a year ago, and 46 percent feel burned out.

- Nearly 40 percent of women are looking for a new job and cited their employer as the reason.

- Just 33 percent of employers offer flexible working policies.

- Ninety-four percent of women feel that asking for more flexibility will affect future promotions.

- Harassment and microaggressions are on the rise and often go unreported (23 percent of microaggressions and 66 percent of harassment).

- Inclusive, supportive organizations gain a competitive advantage in terms of women staying with their employers longer, less burnout and more mental health support.

On a personal note, I had the unfortunately (non)unique experience of being fired for being female. It was in the late '70s, and I was one of two women working at a company. I was working as a receptionist while I looked for a job in my field. The other woman working at this company was a salesperson. One day she told the employer to take their accounts and their job and shove it (not in those terms). That same afternoon I was told to leave because "we can't trust your kind around here." My "kind" meant female. I was too young and inexperienced to know I could have sued.

Being a woman in the workplace continues to have a unique set of challenges. This chapter will give you a few tools to work with.

LEARNING ACTIVITY

Fill in the missing term with the number or statement. Mix and match. Use your pen or pencil.

How Much Do You Know? (Answers in Appendix)

Among S&P 500 companies, researchers found that boards were "gaming diversity" to please potential critics by appointing exactly two women to their boards. Forty-five percent more boards include exactly two women. (Deemed as "_____.")

white privilege

Twelve percent of millennials (35 percent of the US workforce) identify as trans or nonbinary, (double those from Gen X). Cisgender employees make _____ percent more money a year than transgender employees.

20

Women are more likely to be hired with blind applications, which increased the likelihood that a woman would be hired by between 25 and _____ percent.

32

Without diverse leadership, women are _____ percent less likely than straight white men to win endorsement for their ideas.

46

White men who experienced social disadvantages in the workplace based on socioeconomic status, disability, age, sexual orientation or religion are more likely than their white male counterparts who had not experienced such disadvantages to recognize _____.

twokenism

Trends in the Workplace

As Spectra Diversity continues to assess diversity and inclusion at many organizations and universities, we see certain trends occur repeatedly. Some of these trends can be seen in the Annual Spectra Assessment Report available on our website. Consider this:

- Women tend to rate management less favorably than do the men.

- Women and men tend to be similar in the way they rate their organization's culture.

- Women tend to rate their organization's policies, practices and procedures related to D&I more negatively than do the men.

- Women and men are largely the same in their belief systems regarding diversity and inclusion.

- Men tend to rate their interpersonal skills related to D&I higher than do the women.

In addition, a study reported in Forbes found that:

- Seventy-seven percent of women feel there is gender **inequality** in the workplace, compared to 56 percent of men.

- Forty-five percent of men feel that there is already a proactive approach to tackling gender inequality, while 31 percent of women **disagree**.

- When asked whether they are confident that **"by being 'me' at work** I will be able to have the career I want," 67 percent of men agreed, compared to 45 percent of women.

. . . .

"I have felt that certain members of the leadership team treat me differently because I am a woman—being interrupted, being told flat out "Oh, I'm sorry, I wasn't listening" by a male colleague, being asked to repeat myself multiple times (sharing the same info each time) only to have it fall flat until another male colleague repeated what I said and it seemed to land, etc. In general, I think the president has some issues with control and partnering that, with the different way he treats women, I have to imagine a number of the female employees feel as invisible as I do. There have been numerous instances where I've provided information that is in my field of expertise and the president follows up by asking another outside third party (usually men) about the issue to get their version of the same information."

—Anonymous

. . . .

Rebecca is in the unusual position of working in her field first as a man and then as a woman. As a woman she has noticed that she must frequently prove that she knows what she is talking about when she finds a software bug for a large organization—Google, as an example. She also is interrupted now and talked over. That did not happen when she presented as a man.

The bias against women and gender inequity is real.

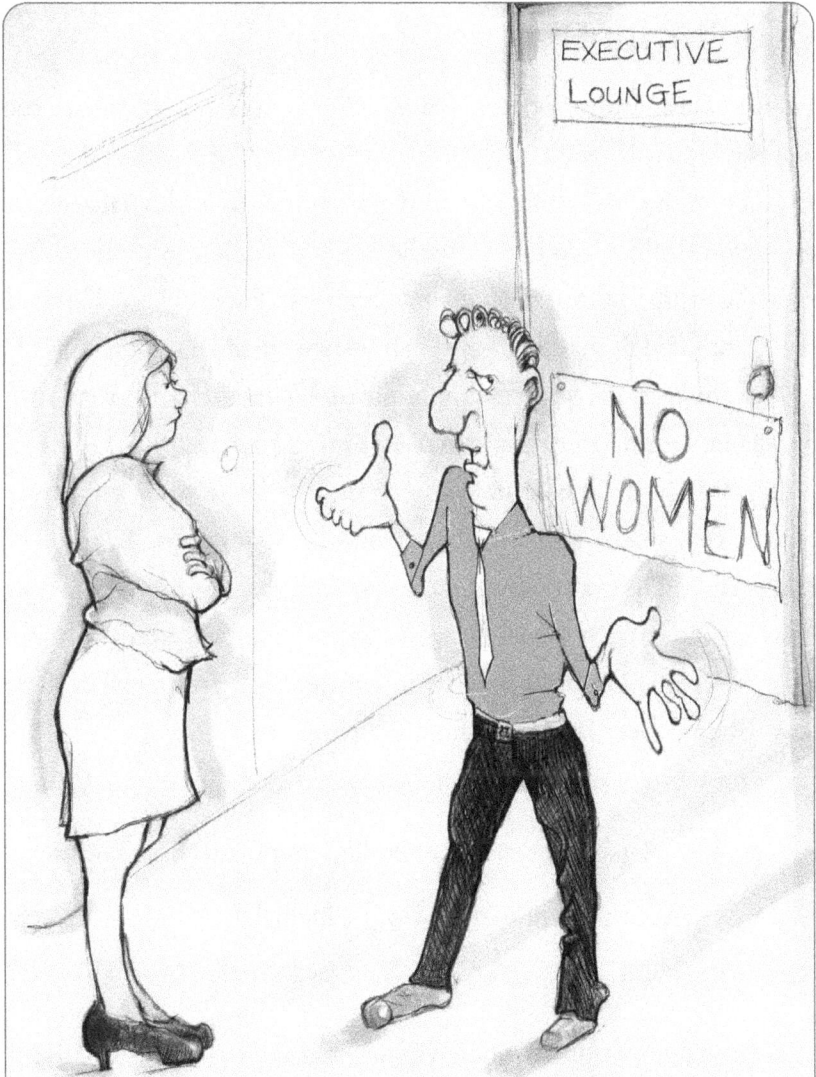

"A glass ceiling?...Don't be ridiculous. The sign works just fine."

Check Your Bias

Howard Ross, author of *Reinventing Diversity*, states that "we see the world not as it is, but as we are."

When the "we" doing the hiring are primarily male managers, it can become difficult to see bias in the process. Women continue to face a "broken rung" at the first step up to manager. For every one hundred men promoted to manager, only eighty-six women are promoted.

If you're not concerned about women in the workplace in a pandemic world, you should be. According to a Deloitte report in 2022, **"More than half of women plan to leave their employer within two years."** This is most pronounced for those in middle-management and nonmanagerial roles, with fewer than one-quarter of women in those roles planning to stay with their employer for more than two years. **Only 10 percent of women plan to stay with their current employer for more than five years**.

The main reasons women left their former employer were as follows:

- Twenty-two percent—not enough opportunities to advance

- Eighteen percent—lack of work/life balance

- Eighteen percent—pay wasn't high enough.

The main reasons women are considering leaving their current employer are:

- Thirty-eight percent—feel burned out

- Twenty-seven percent—pay isn't high enough

- Thirteen percent—not enough opportunities to advance

Here is a simple checklist to see if your bias is holding women back during the hiring process.

LEARNING ACTIVITY

Make a check mark in the Yes or No column.

ACTION	YES— I'VE DONE THIS	NO— I HAVEN'T DONE THIS
Conduct exit interviews to determine why "good" hires leave, and look for a gender pattern.		
Check job application forms to eliminate gender bias.		
Hide name and gender on application forms that are reviewed by HR or the hiring manager.		
Look for sources of new employees beyond referrals and internal sources.		
Standardize the interview questions, and ask the same ones in the same order, every time.		
Add diversity to the hiring process. Have interviewers of more than one gender (race/ethnicity, age, ability) during in-person or online interviews.		
Include a statement of inclusion to your hiring process to make public your organization's DEI policy.		
Question your assumptions if an applicant "doesn't seem like a good fit." Ask yourself why?		
Switch from pay "range" to a set salary for specific jobs. Men tend to overestimate skills, and women tend to underestimate.		
Take your time. Quick hires can lead to gut impulses.		

Ten boxes checked: Congratulations. Diversity and inclusion are probably part of everyday business and are fully integrated and part of the cultural norms of the organization. Your organization has its diversity and inclusion best practices emulated by other organizations.

Nine boxes checked: You're ahead of the curve. You're a role model for other organizations. It's likely the policies, practices and procedures at your organization are inclusive. Employees are committed to diversity and see themselves as responsible for creating a culture that is inclusive for all.

Three to eight boxes checked: You're in the middle of the pack. You probably have measurements in place to evaluate diversity and inclusion initiatives. There is some infrastructure (e.g., diversity and inclusion council, employee resource groups, etc.). Diversity and inclusion are aligned with the organization's mission and vision. You're working to promote inclusion.

Two boxes checked: You have a lot of opportunity to change your ways. Perhaps you follow basic federally mandated antidiscrimination laws to avoid negative consequences. Your focus is on treating everyone the same way.

One box checked: For you, diversity and inclusion are not seen as a real issue. Your organization may lack policies and procedures to address diversity and inclusion. The work atmosphere may feel hostile to employees who are perceived as different.

Reducing Bias when Hiring

When it comes to bias in the hiring process, there is a famous example within professional symphony orchestras. Prior to the 1950s, many orchestras invited new members to join based on the conductor's recommendations. In the 1950s several top-rated symphony orchestras began using blind auditions. In a blind audition, the person being auditioned played his or her instrument while hidden behind a screen. Think of the TV program *The Voice* and you have a decent idea of how it would work. Only the instrument and its player were being judged.

The rate of women in these orchestras went from 6 percent in 1970 to 21 percent in 1993. When you consider that a musician's tenure in an orchestra can span decades, this increase was significant. It still wasn't enough, however, to eliminate the bias in favor of men. In recent years, the blind auditioners are asked to walk across the stage (behind the curtain) in stocking feet. Apparently, the click-click-click of women's heels was a giveaway to the gender of the auditioner.

An additional anonymization study was conducted on the applicants to work on the Hubble Space Telescope. Before any anonymization, men outperformed women by about 5 percent. After just the removal of the names, that number dropped to less than 3 percent. When the applications were fully anonymized, women outperformed men by 1 percent.

It takes effort and often policy changes to reduce gender bias when hiring and promoting. One of the first steps is the application form. There are certain words that become bias code for the type of person you're looking for. The following are a few tips from Glassdoor.

- **Limit the lingo.** Avoid including words in your titles like "hacker," "rockstar," "superhero," "guru," and "ninja," and use neutral, descriptive titles like "engineer," "project manager," or "developer."

- **Say no to adjectives.** Avoid superlatives such as "expert," "superior" and "world class." These terms can turn off female candidates who tend to be more collaborative than competitive in nature.

- **Is education that important?** Reconsider the requirement of specific majors. Glassdoor Economic Research found that the choice of college major can vary by gender, so you may be limiting your candidate pool by unnecessarily requiring completion of a specific degree. This one rings especially true for this author, who is a theater and mass communications graduate running a DEI technology company.

- **Eliminate gender leaning words.** Avoid gender specific terms such as "crush it" or "dominate." "Analyze" and "determine" are typically associated with male traits, while "collaborate" and "support" are considered female.

Three Quick Tips to Overcome Bias during the Interview

1. Have more than one person present during interviews.

2. Ask the same questions every time, in the same order.

3. Use a rubric for two interviewers to take notes during the interview—then compare notes.

There are a few tools you can use to automate the process of looking for gender associations in your job applications. Textio is a fee-for-service tool that analyzes the language you use in your job applications. Textio is a flexible and reasonably priced tool. A free tool you can use is Gender Decoder. You simply paste your ad copy in the tool and view the results.

· ·

"I think one key step to help make our organization feel more inclusive and equitable is to ensure equitable treatment of female employees—even on things as small as basic meeting etiquette—like don't interrupt your female staff more than your male staff, don't show up late to meetings

run by female staff and then try to assume control of the
meeting, don't immediately repeat a female colleagues
opinions/contributions as though they needed reexplain-
ing, don't ask your female employees to repeat themselves
multiple times, implying you don't believe they are right
(but then 'believing' the same information when shared by a
male) and so on."

—Anonymous

Why Women? The Business Case

If we have demonstrated that women have a harder time at work, experience more burnout and are subject to more bias—why does it benefit an organization to have more women? And specifically, more women in leadership?

There are many reasons. Here are ten reasons why you should include women in your hiring and in leadership.

1. Having women at the C-suite level significantly increases net margins. A one-percentage-point increase in women represents a 15 percent boost to profitability.

2. Companies that have women in top management roles experience what we call "innovation intensity" and produce more patents—by an average of 20 percent more than teams with male leaders.

3. Having female senior leaders creates less gender discrimination in recruitment, promotion and retention, according to the Peterson Institute.

4. Women add needed perspective and decision-making. A study at Penn Medicine found greater neural connectivity from front to back and within one hemisphere in males, suggesting their brains are structured to facilitate connectivity between perception and coordinated action. In contrast, in females, the wiring goes between the left and right hemispheres, suggesting that they facilitate communication between the analytical and intuition. In other words, men are wired for action and women are wired for collaboration. You want to have both in your management team.

5. Fifty-nine percent of Americans believe women business leaders show more compassion and empathy than men. This can translate into employee engagement, satisfaction and retention.

6. When women are in your organization, you gain better reflection of a wider customer base, which leads to market share and higher profits. There are more female than male consumers who could potentially use your organization's products or services.

7. Compared to men in similar positions, women managers are consistently doing more to promote employee well-being. This includes checking on team members, helping them manage workloads and providing support for those who are dealing with burnout or navigating work/life challenges.

8. Women are more likely to support DEI initiatives—the benefits of which we've already seen. Thirty-eight percent of senior-level women mentor or sponsor at least one

woman of color, compared to only 26 percent of senior-level men.

9. In the last chapter we learned about the importance of emotional intelligence in leadership roles. Studies show that women outperform men in eleven of twelve key emotional intelligence competencies.

10. Trust. According to the Pew Research Center's Women and Leadership survey, 34 percent of American workers say that women have an edge over men when it comes to being honest and ethical, while just 3 percent believe men are better.

Dos and Don'ts for Inclusion of Underrepresented Genders

There are several actions you can take to recruit, promote and retain women and transgender people in your organization. Here are a few things to do and not to do.

Take These Actions

- Expand your recruitment beyond networking with your existing employees.

- Use gender-neutral language in your job postings.

- Encourage the use of proper gender pronouns in the workplace.

- Set up a mentorship program to help women succeed in the workplace.

- Make managers accountable for gender equity and accountability in their KPIs and other metrics.

- Create an employee resource group for women (more on this in chapter 3).

- Listen without judgment when issues of bias, microaggressions or harassment are brought to your attention; then take appropriate, gender-affirming and inclusive action.

Avoid These Actions

- DON'T make gender pronouns mandatory in email signatures and name badges.

- DON'T hire using salary ranges; use a fixed salary instead.

- DON'T assign the "extra" duties (note taking, snacks, kitchen cleanup) to women. Rotate between all team members.

- DON'T promote from within without making the promotion available to all.

- DON'T hire based on a good fit for the corporate culture. This is Assimilation 101. In fact, the term *culture fit* undermines the very foundation of DEI work. A change in culture may be just what you need.

- DON'T make any decision about BIPOC women without BIPOC women at the table.

- DON'T dump gender-bias issues onto the women in your leadership. Men need to be involved.

ACTION ITEMS

❑ Measure the perceptions of your female employees so you know what you're doing right and where you can improve. This means gathering both the qualitative data (words, opinions) and the quantitative data (facts, statistics).

❑ Change your talent life cycle policies, practices and procedures as needed to be gender neutral in job descriptions, interviews, salaries and promotions.

❑ Set goals to increase the participation of women in leadership to achieve parity.

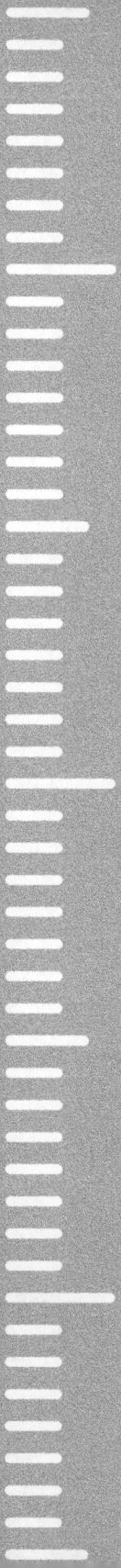

CHAPTER 5

Are People of Color Underrepresented in Your Company?

Darkness cannot drive out darkness; only light can do that. Hate cannot drive out hate; only love can do that.

—MARTIN LUTHER KING JR.

Start with Measurement

CASE STUDY: International Nonprofit Organization

A colleague of mine, Tawana Bhagwat of Organization at Its Best (OAIB), is a DEI consultant. She begins her DEI relationship with her clients by using an assessment. *"The assessment is a baseline to gather the quantitative data. We also do stakeholder interviews to gather the qualitative data. It's a baseline, and it also warms up the organization for the strategy that will come next," said Tawana.*

One of her clients is a global nonprofit organization with 3,500 employees in the United States, and all others are in Africa.

"Based on the assessment and the interviews, we identified five areas that we wanted to focus on, and that led to the strategy work," said Tawana.

Those areas included communications, talent management and decentralization of decision-making. They put a road map together with strategies that led to specific actions and deliverables, which led to KPIs.

As she was preparing to use the Spectra Assessment and speaking with the stakeholders, she found the demographic data gathering wasn't quite working for Africa.

"I learned the demographics are coming from a US lens and the people on the continent were saying, 'That doesn't work well. All of us are Black. So, what are we talking about?' And so, really, that colonization lens and tribalism and regionalism needed to be accounted for," said Tawana.

In fact, the demographics we collect in the US don't work in most of the world. For this nonprofit organization, OAIB collected the traditional US race and ethnicity data, as well as custom categories using geographic regions.

The organization is 55 percent Black / African American, 32 percent white, 5 percent Asian / Asian American and the remainder is other or multiracial. They are primarily women (54 percent), and 45 percent are between the ages of 45–54.

Why doesn't the collection of race data work other than in the United States?

Because race is a social construct.

There Is No Such Thing as Race

Race is a social construct. We don't have Black blood, Asian blood or white blood. We have human blood that is type A, A+, AB, O and other types. Our skin color isn't black or white. It is gradations of black,

114

brown, beige and ivory. We have external characteristics that place us in social groups. Hair can be curly or straight; eyes blue or brown. These are geographic characteristics that emerged over millennia in response to climate and other geographic factors. These observable differences place us within a racial group in the United States.

Continuum of Race

Race in millions

Black	Indigenous	AAPI	Multiracial	White
46.9	9.7	25.6	33.8	204.3

According to the 2020 Census there is a continuum of race in the United States as shown on the previous page.

Notice there is no category for Hispanic or Latinx in the US racial census. Hispanic/Latinx is tracked separately from the race category. I spoke recently to a Black woman who is from Panama. She considers herself both Black and Hispanic. Many people fall into this multicultural, multiracial category.

Being Jewish is also not included in the US census as a race. Some people describe it as a religion, and others as a race and still others define Jewishness as both a religion and a race. Ninety-two percent of Jewish Americans identify as white.

Continuum of Race

Race in reality %

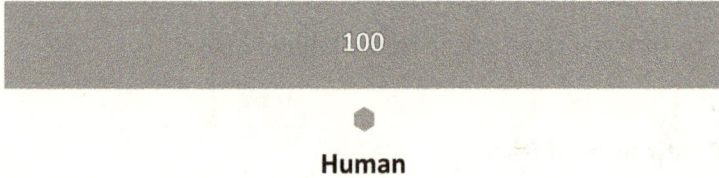

100

Human

Under the skin, there is no biological difference that can be termed *race*. All human beings are 99.9 percent identical in their genetic makeup. In 1859, Charles Darwin wrote in the opening pages of *On the Origin of Species*, "the view which most naturalists entertain, and which I formerly entertained, namely that each species has been independently created—is erroneous." Sadly, his offer of natural selection was used soon after as another method to biologically distinguish and rank the races.

The social construct of race is very real in the US. We have physical and social differences and adopt our in-group and our out-group by the age of three. To learn how it became so ingrained in our culture, we must take a step into our history. An extremely condensed timeline of who was in the "out-group" according to the dominant white male group can be found on page 118.

The manifesto posted by the accused mass murderer in a Buffalo, New York, grocery store (May 14, 2022) promoted the "Great Replacement Theory." This racist conspiracy narrative falsely asserts there is an active, ongoing and covert effort to replace white populations in current white-majority countries.

"Actually, we're just getting started."

US History of Racist Behavior

- 1500s—Arrival of Europeans to the Americas. Indigenous people are the "other" race (out-group). Genocide begins.

- 1619—Slaves are brought by Europeans to the Americas.

- 1790—Benjamin Franklin petitions Congress to abolish slavery. One month later, the Naturalization Act of 1790 limits citizenship to whites.

- 1848—The Mexican Cession is the region in the modern-day southwestern United States that Mexico ceded to the US in the Treaty of Guadalupe Hidalgo after the Mexican–American War.

- 1912—Mexicans in New Mexico receive full US citizenship after the state's admission to the Union. Whites of Forsyth County, Georgia, violently drive out nearly 1,100 of their Black neighbors.

- 1920—The Nineteenth Amendment gives women the right to vote. Most African American women, like African American men, are prevented from voting in Southern states.

- 1923—*United States v. Bhagat Singh Thind* was a case in which the Supreme Court decided that Bhagat Singh Thind, an Indian Sikh man who identified himself as an Aryan (from the Caucasus Mountains), was ineligible for naturalized citizenship in the United States. He was not "Caucasian" in the eyes of the court.

- 1935—The National Labor Relations Act guarantees the right to organize and form unions. The Act excludes farm and domestic jobs, historically held by African Americans and Latinos.

- 1942—The Bracero Program invites Mexican citizens to work temporarily in the US. That same year, President Roosevelt authorizes mass internment of more than 120,000 Japanese American citizens and documented immigrants.

- 1954—In *Brown v. Board of Education*, the Supreme Court unanimously rules segregation in public schools as unconstitutional. The Immigration and Naturalization Service institutes Operation Wetback to deport undocumented Mexicans living in the US.

- 1955—Rosa Parks keeps her seat on a bus. Emmett Till is murdered for whistling at white woman who, decades later, will admit to false testimony.

- 1963—Approximately 250,000 attend the March on Washington, hear Martin Luther King Jr. deliver the "I Have a Dream" speech. Ku Klux Klan members bomb the 16th Street Baptist Church in Birmingham, Alabama, killing four Black girls in Sunday school.

- 1964—President Johnson signs the Civil Rights Act of 1964, outlawing discrimination based on race, color, religion, sex and national origin. Civil rights workers Michael Schwerner, James Chaney and Andrew Goodman are murdered by the KKK in Mississippi.

- 1967—In *Loving v. Virginia*, the Supreme Court rules prohibiting interracial marriage as unconstitutional. During the "long, hot summer" of 1967, race riots erupt across the US, killing dozens, injuring thousands and setting the stage for historic violence in 1968.

- 2009—Sonia Sotomayor becomes the first Latina Supreme Court justice. Harvard professor, renowned scholar Henry Louis Gates Jr., a Black man, is arrested on suspicion of breaking and entering—at his own home.

- 2017—Federal courts halt enforcement of President Trump's order effectively banning Muslim immigrants from seven countries.

- 2022—Justice Ketanji Brown Jackson becomes the first Black woman confirmed as a Supreme Court justice. Also in 2022, there are 733 documented hate groups, 98 white nationalist groups and 5,680 white supremacist flyering incidents. (A *flyering incident* is the posting of banners or flyers promoting hate, white supremacy and other similar beliefs.)

Where Is Your Starting Line?

In your organization, are the BIPOC employees referred to as a "diversity hire" or "diversity candidate"? If so, this can be felt as a deeply offensive, company-sanctioned racial microaggression. The company is virtue signaling to all employees that whiteness is prized and prioritized.

As you read the above timeline, did you think, "But I wasn't even born yet! I didn't do any of that. It's not my fault."

Most of it was before my time as well. I didn't cause systemic racism. But I've also never been followed in a store by the clerk because of my skin color. I've never been denied a place to live because of my race. I can walk into a private golf club to use the restroom because it is convenient, even though I'm not a member. I'm not terrified when pulled over for a traffic violation as I decide whether to flirt or cry. I have privilege as a white woman, even though as a white woman I have less privilege than a white man.

A few years ago, I was working at Notre Dame on a video program about safety. It covered all types of safety—religious, sexual, racial and personal property, to name a few. I interviewed several students for this project. One Black female student told me about her freshman year dorm assignment. She didn't know anyone else going to the university, so she had a random assignment. This woman happened to be tall, and her new (white) roommate asked her if she was there on a basketball or volleyball scholarship. The assumption was apparently that only Black athletes attend the school. The Black student *was* there on a scholarship, as it happened—for mathematics.

The average Black college student must achieve many more accomplishments and overcome barriers even before entering college compared to the average white student. At the time of college graduation, Black students typically have more debt than a white student—and many don't earn degrees at all because of financial hardship rather than academic shortcomings.

. . . .

"Unlearning white privilege is hard. I've found it challenging to recognize the extent to which I must think more carefully before I speak or email to avoid the possibility of giving unintended offense, and I don't like being afraid to speak. But I tell myself this is what African Americans and immigrants have gone through for hundreds of years, and it's what unlearning white privilege is all about."

—Anonymous

. . . .

LEARNING ACTIVITY

In Spectra Diversity's diversity and inclusion training, there is an exercise called the "privilege walk." In it, people start by standing in a horizontal line across the room, like a starting line. The facilitator then begins reading statements and asking participants to take a step forward or back, depending on their answer to the statement.

You can try this by standing up in the room you're in—and stepping forward or back. Here are ten of the statements:

1. If your ancestors were forced against their will to come to the USA, step back.

2. If your primary ethnic identity is US American, step forward.

3. If your family employed people in your household as domestic workers, step forward.

4. If you were often ashamed or embarrassed of your material possessions, step back.

5. If most of your family members worked in careers requiring a college education, step forward.

6. If you were raised in an area where there was visible prostitution or drug activity, step back.

7. If you studied the cultures of your ancestors in elementary school, step forward.

8. If you started school speaking a language other than English, step back.

9. If there were more than one hundred books in your home when you grew up, step forward.

10. If you ever had to skip a meal or go hungry because there was not enough money to buy food when you were growing up, step back.

Are you where you started? Did you move forward or back?

By the end of forty statements, participants are clearly and visually separated by those who had/have unearned privilege in their lives and those who had/have less privilege. The participants in the back of the room are not surprised by how far back they are. They have lived the experience. The people who are surprised are the people in the front of the room. Many feel guilty. Nearly all are surprised. To see their unearned privilege in such a visceral way can be shocking and upsetting.

The issue isn't that white people didn't work hard to get to where they are. The issue is that a BIPOC person and a white person have different starting lines.

Everyone living today has a responsibility to halt systemic racism and work for racial equity in the workplace, at home and in the community. It's not enough to be nonracist. Becoming antiracist is a better goal.

· ·

"Casual racisms are very prominent, and workers are not being forced to address their unconscious bias beliefs. To improve, this would need to be addressed. For example, when homeowners who are predominantly People of Color have worked at the store, they are delegated to work in the back and clean furniture, instead of using them for other skills they might have. Many are bilingual, which would be extremely useful at the cashier station at the store, but the manager has them continuously working in the back."

—Anonymous

· ·

LEARNING ACTIVITY

How Much Do You Know (Answers in Appendix)

Mix and match. Get your pen or pencil out.

_____ percent of Generation Z are racial or ethnic minorities.	65
People who identify as "white non-Hispanic" in the United States declined in numbers for the first time on record, falling below 58 percent of the country's population in 2020.	48
By 20__, the US population will not have any single ethnic or racial majorities.	58
_____ percent of companies on the S&P 500 do not have at least one Black board member. Today, there are five Black CEOs in the Fortune 500.	24
Without diverse leadership, People of Color are _____ less likely than straight white men to win endorsement for their ideas.	29.6

Busting the Diversity Myths

The Pipeline Myth: "There Are Not Enough [Fill in the Blank] Candidates"

One of the first ways to ensure you have enough racially and ethnically diverse candidates in your internal and external pipeline is to audit your previous job applications. Use the analysis tool from the previous chapter to make sure those with gender and race/ethnic diversity and intersectionality are included in your potential pool. *Intersectionality*, a word created by Kimberlé Crenshaw, is the combination of our demographic traits. Using myself as an example, I am a white cisgender woman with an invisible disability. You could be a white gay man or a Black cisgender man. We are all more than one demographic and cultural trait.

Next, measure your organization.

- Where did your previous hires come from?

- If they were referrals, were they from the dominant group (white?) in your organization?

- Do you know what your organization's dominant group is in terms of demographics?

- Are your BIPOC employees in your network system for new hires *and* for promotions?

A third tactic you can use is to look into advertising and networking with nontraditional groups, such as your local Black, Hispanic and Asian chambers of commerce.

If your organization states that you follow EEOC guidelines, that isn't enough. That is the bare minimum.

The Ivy League Myth: "We Only Recruit from Top Schools"

Women outnumber men in achievement of associate's, bachelor's and master's degrees as well as doctorates. There are no doubt women of color who are graduating from any school you choose.

Look at the numbers:

- There are 69,852 male Ivy Leagues students.

- There are 76,999 female Ivy League students.

- Ivy League graduation rate is 96.13 percent.

- HBCUs (historically Black colleges and universities) have 228,000 students—more than the Ivy Leagues.

- HBCU graduation rate is comparable to other colleges and universities nationwide.

- HBCUs make up 3 percent of the colleges and universities in the US and produce nearly 20 percent of all Black graduates.

- Among 31,640 doctoral candidates, 57.8 percent are white, 16.7 percent are Hispanic, 11.5 percent are Asian and 6 percent are LGBTQ.

Would you rather have one of the few Ivy League candidates who graduated at the middle or bottom of their class, or a top student from an HBCU or other school? By limiting your candidate pool to Ivy Leagues, you are limiting the number of highly qualified individuals who could be your best employees. Remember, research shows that educational qualifications do not have a significant effect on job performance.

The chart below is from data shown at the Diversity Inclusion Research Conference held in 2021. The data suggests you'd increase your talent pipeline significantly if you looked in places *other* than one of the top-tier schools.

Check Your Math

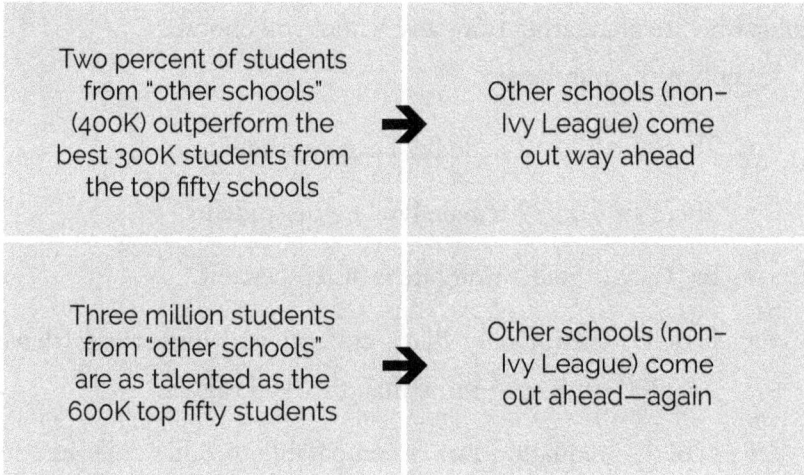

Two percent of students from "other schools" (400K) outperform the best 300K students from the top fifty schools **→**	Other schools (non–Ivy League) come out way ahead
Three million students from "other schools" are as talented as the 600K top fifty students **→**	Other schools (non–Ivy League) come out ahead—again

Would you prefer a pool of six hundred graduating seniors—or three million? The way I've always viewed it, a degree shows that you're trainable. On-the-job training ends up being the way of the world for many degreed employees.

The "We Don't Want to Lower the Bar" Myth

"Lowering the bar" assumes that there is an actual bar to be lowered. Does your organization have minimum standards for each job description? As mentioned earlier, Bill Gates was only a high school graduate. Would you have "lowered the bar" to hire him? The location of the bar says as much about the interviewer and the organization as it does about the applicants.

The idea that there are no qualified applicants who are also BIPOC is a false one. It is closely related to the concept that organizations (or universities) hire (or accept) individuals who are minorities to fulfill some type of numerical quota. It is the belief that affirmative action rewards gender and race at the expense of merit. The reality is that it would be unlawful to do so. Under Title VII of the Civil Rights Act, you cannot base a hiring decision, in whole or in part, on a person's race or gender.

So—there is no quota. You don't have to lower the bar. You simply need to expand your horizons to include people other than the usual suspects.

The Meritocracy Myth: "Anyone Can Get to the Top"

"Our culture is very results oriented. We have a strong focus on developing and delivering important therapies to patients in need. This leads to a significant meritocracy approach, combined with a scientific attitude that embraces diversity of opinion in formative processes, but can result in a perception that decisions are overly top down (and sometimes heavy handed). To the extent that we have DEI challenges, it is driven by a "color blind" approach we have used historically that limits our ability to optimally create an inclusive environment or to address unconscious biases."

—Anonymous

Those who began the race of life at the white starting line (remember the privilege walk?) may believe that they got to where they are by hard work. And maybe a little luck. *If you want to succeed, you just need to work hard.* Sadly, meritocracy is a myth.

Michael J. Sandel wrote, "Our disagreements about merit are not only about fairness. They are also about how we define success and failure, winning and losing—and about the attitudes the winners should hold toward those less successful than themselves. These are highly charged questions, and we try to avoid them until they force themselves upon us. Finding our way beyond the polarized politics of our time requires a reckoning with merit. How has its meaning been recast in recent decades, in ways that erode the dignity of work and leave many people feeling that elites look down on them? Are the winners of globalization justified in the belief that they have earned and therefore deserve their success, or is this a matter of meritocratic hubris?"

> "There is no need for more D&I. This is a propaganda tool meant to subvert people and hire less competent people and divide them … I do not agree to hire people who are just needed based on their sexuality or color etc. preference but rather on their capability of delivering their mental capabilities to the company and doing the job right. This is a dangerous time for us to start rewriting laws that fits the insane; it will divide the people even more greatly and lower our standards in the company."
>
> **—Anonymous**

The Insight Center for Community Economic Development published a report stating that white people have benefited from government help in the past and have been able to create generational wealth through homeownership and other means.

- The Homestead Act of 1862 helped white Americans settle the West (and push out the Indigenous population). The US government distributed 270 million acres of land to 1.5 million white families, 45 million of whom still benefit from that land today.

- When the Emancipation Proclamation was signed, 0.5 percent of the US's total wealth was in the hands of Black people. Today, that figure is 1–2 percent.

- The GI Bill, key to building the white middle class, provided $190 billion in federal loans for nearly 2.4 million veterans returning from World War II. Black veterans were largely excluded.

- Black heads of household with a college degree hold $22,000 less wealth than their white counterparts with high school diplomas.

Meritocracy in college admissions had a scandal a few years ago when several parents were caught cheating to get their children into the desired schools. Trials were held, and a few people went to jail. Sadly, this is not uncommon. "The lengths that families went to in the Varsity Blues scandal—one allegedly paid $6.5 million to get a child into Stanford—highlight just how unusual outright illegal corruption remains."

This provides further insight into the argument to look beyond the Ivy Leagues schools when hiring.

The Geography Myth:
"Our Community Is Very White"

In my experience, this is a common excuse. I live in a predominantly white state and sing in a majority-white choir. I've been advocating for a while to diversify our choir by having joint concerts with a Black choir and by other means. An excuse was given that "We represent the demographics of our white suburb." Except that isn't true. The white suburb that our choir is in, is 86.2 percent white. Our choir is 98 percent white.

At Spectra Diversity, we see trends in data all the time. One trend, as in the above example, is that organizations that are mainly white say that they can't have more diversity among their ranks because they "are in a white state, city or region." When they see the comparisons, it is often eye opening. Below are two comparisons, representing a city and a state. National comparisons show similar results.

WASHINGTON DC— SURVEYED ORGANIZATION DEMOGRAPHICS	WASHINGTON DC— DEMOGRAPHIC REALITY
White—69% Black—19% Asian—7% Hispanic—2% Multiracial—2% Other—2%	White—37% Black—46% Asian—4% Hispanic—5% Multiracial—3% Other—5%
IOWA—SURVEYED ORGANIZATION'S DEMOGRAPHICS	IOWA—DEMOGRAPHIC REALITY
White—93% Black—1% Asian—1% Hispanic—3% Other/Multiracial—2%	White—87% Black—4% Asian—3% Hispanic—6%

It would be simple to check your organization's demographics against your city, region or state—if you collect racial data. Ask your HR department for any racial data they may have, and let Google tell you the geographic demographics. Where do you stand? **Measure it!**

People can argue about diversity, equity and inclusion and have their own opinions. It is hard to argue with facts.

"Microaggressive behavior from white people, men and older/more tenured staff is a major diversity and inclusion challenge I've had, as well as having a leadership that is not representative of my most salient identities. I'm also often forced to speak on behalf of *all* Black people and *all* People of Color as if we exist in a monolith. Additionally, because of people's biases, networking and fostering professional relationships is difficult when I'm in spaces that aren't diverse and therefore full of people who do not look like me."

—Anonymous

Workplace Strategies to Mitigate Systemic Racism

Hiring for diversity isn't about meeting a quota. It's about giving BIPOC individuals a fair shot. Below are a few tips.

- Measure your employees' current diversity, equity and inclusion (DEI) beliefs and interpersonal behaviors.

- Tailor a strategic DEI plan to fit your organization's unique needs. Many plans include unconscious bias awareness sessions, executive listening sessions and interpersonal skills training related to DEI. Your plan could/should include:

- employee resource groups (ERGs) used as discussion and action groups aligned around a particular topic or demographic;

- DEI council to provide input to leadership and decision-makers;

- chief diversity officer, if you don't already have one;

- DEI lens on your organization's hiring and other policies, practices and procedures; and

- DEI policy known to your employees and made public to your key stakeholders and customers.

- Execute on the plan, and measure again.

CASE STUDY Part Deux:
International Nonprofit Organization

Earlier in this chapter we began the story of an international nonprofit organization. Here is the rest of the story.

Using the results from the Spectra Assessment, Organization at Its Best (OAIB) went through the qualitative and quantitative data and "put a road map together where those strategies were matched with specific actions, deliverables and measures, KPI and resources next to each one of those. And we reviewed it with our leadership team. One of the critical items that came out of that was that they needed a dedicated EBITDA," said Tawana Bhagwat.

EBITDA, or earnings before interest, taxes, depreciation and amortization, is a valuable way to measure a company's financial health and ability to generate cash flow. If you understand and apply EBITDA, you can uncover your business's value while assessing your company's performance. Diversity, equity and inclusion within your organization is a proven way to increase profitability and innovation, as we're demonstrating in this book.

OAIB also went through the organization's handbook with an equity lens and revised almost thirty of their policies. Revising policies can be a quick and visible fix to show your employees that your diversity, equity and inclusion efforts are not a passing fad. In addition, OAIB trained about one-third of the organization. They also helped create ERGs. Now each work team has some activity that they're actively doing once a month.

"So, they really are proactively trying to create a psychologically safe space, but also raising awareness, educating by taking it on at a personal level, not just waiting for the organization to do some big brand activity," said Tawana.

The organization's managers get an update about how they're progressing. They're currently planning on a reassessment one year after their first use of the Spectra Assessment.

"The first assessment was a baseline. We're planning a new assessment for measurement during 2022," said Tawana.

Assessments aren't a one-and-done. You execute an assessment—create the DEI strategy—and measure again. Diversity and inclusion are a journey—not a destination.

"Our standards are very high. We even have high double standards."

Managing Resistance

As you work on your diversity, equity and inclusion journey, your organization will no doubt have resistance to your efforts—at either the leadership level or the employee level. Spectra Diversity's assessments show that Black employees tend to rate management, policies, practices and procedures less favorably than white employees in nearly all small- and medium-size organizations. Consider this:

- As of May 2020, the Hispanic unemployment rate was highest at 17.6 percent, followed by the Black unemployment rate at 16.8 percent, the Asian unemployment rate at 15.0 percent and the white unemployment rate at 12.4 percent.

- A 2016 study by Sonia Kang and colleagues found that "31% of the Black professionals and 40% of the Asian professionals they interviewed admitted to 'whitening' their résumés, by either adopting a less 'ethnic' name or omitting extracurricular experiences (a college club membership, for instance) that might reveal their racial identities."

- African Americans are 50 percent less likely to receive callbacks compared to white candidates.

"I know that diversity and inclusion typically don't apply to white people, and I do understand that I likely carry bias just by virtue of being white. However, I am not privileged, and I don't appreciate being berated for being white or female. I make every effort to write in a way that is inclusive—and several other People of Color had reviewed my work and called it remarkable."

—Anonymous

The benefits are clear. Organizations that are diverse are

- 70 percent more likely to capture new markets,
- 75 percent faster time to market,
- 19 percent higher innovation revenue and
- 120 percent more likely to hit financial goals.

Additionally,

- 87 percent of the time, diverse and inclusive teams make better decisions, and
- 87 percent of the Most Admired companies see positive impact of diversity and inclusions in business performance.

Your Name Is So Hard to Pronounce. I'll Just Call You Judy.

. . . .

"I have had a white colleague take my idea for a project and present it as hers. I sat in a meeting with white colleagues (before COVID-19) in a conference room that, while colleagues in our country were presenting, mute the line to say that they don't understand them and make remarks that were derogatory."

—Anonymous

. . . .

This is a short little test. Have you heard (or said) any of the following comments? If you have, they indicate there's some diversity and inclusion work to do in your organization.

- I was taught to treat everyone the same.

- I don't care if someone is pink, purple or polka dotted.

- We're all just a different shade of brown.

- I have a Black friend, so I understand where you're coming from.

- My parents weren't racist, so that's why I'm not racist.

- Focusing on race is what divides us.

- If people are respectful of me, I'll be respectful of them.

- I was white and picked on because I was poor, so I don't have race privilege.

- I'm not racist. I'm from Canada.

According to McKinsey & Company, at the current rate of progress, it will take **twenty-nine years** for the average US company to reach gender parity on its executive team and eighteen years on boards. That's at least one full generation. If you consider the intersectionality of gender *and* race, the picture is even more bleak. A Pew Research poll found more than 80 percent of Black respondents say the legacy of slavery continues to affect the lives of modern Black people, including 59 percent who said it affects them "a great deal."

Spectra Diversity did a psychometric analysis to see where there were statistical differences between men/women/nonbinary/third gender and race/ethnicity in regards to employee views of management. The chart below is based on a five-point Likert scale for a possible 5–25 points.

You can see that the most positive impressions (the higher level of agreement) are held by white men. The lowest opinion (lower level of agreement) was held by white nonbinary / third-gender individuals. Their starting line was probably farther back.

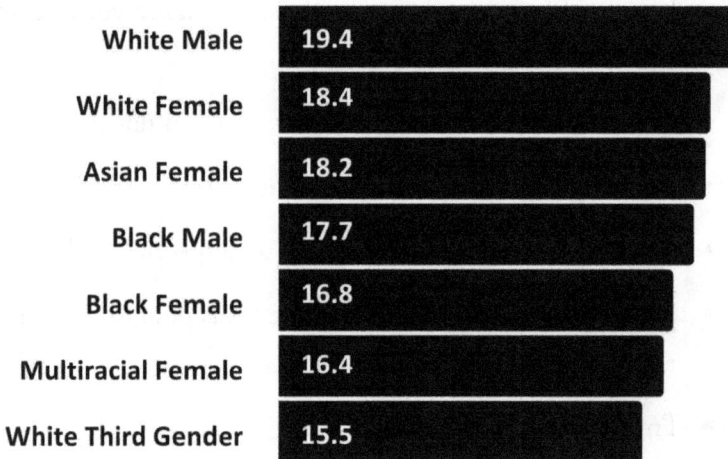

White Male	19.4
White Female	18.4
Asian Female	18.2
Black Male	17.7
Black Female	16.8
Multiracial Female	16.4
White Third Gender	15.5

Systemic racism is residue from the past that affects both our present and future. You may have heard about redlining, the practice of not selling homes or approving mortgages in specific geographic areas to any race or ethnicity other than white. The residue from that practice can be seen today in our segregated neighborhoods.

Another systemic racism practice you may not have heard of is a racial covenant. Kevin Ehrman-Solberg, the son of one of my friends, died accidentally at the youthful age of thirty-three. Kevin had one semester left toward his PhD at the University of Minnesota. He was well known nationally for his groundbreaking work on the Mapping Prejudice project. The project looked at how racially restrictive covenants attached to thousands of homes in Minneapolis during the early 1900s created the Black sections of the city that remain today. Its website has a timeline map where you can view the growth of racially restricted areas up until the 1950s. Those covenants remain in place today. Kevin gave a TED Talk on the topic of race, privilege and mapping.

"During a group meeting in which our work in the UK came up, people were joking around about how small England is and laughingly wondering how it became such a powerful country. I was painfully aware that the answer is colonialism and slavery and was worried about how my colleagues of color were feeling in that moment."

—Anonymous

Ethnic names also remain a problem. Two decades ago, a Black woman named Kalisha White applied for a team leader position at Target and worried that her application had been ignored because of her race. She sent it back in with a **different name** and slightly **fewer qualifications**. That application, with a whitish name and less experience, got her an interview. She filed a class-action lawsuit and won.

A recent study conducted by the University of California, Berkeley and the University of Chicago sent applications to 108 Fortune 500 employers. Half had white-sounding names and the other half had distinctively Black-sounding names. Applicants with Black names were called back 10 percent fewer times across the board despite having comparable applications to their white counterparts.

And now, imagine having your given name changed by your manager, because they had trouble pronouncing it.

"I'll never remember the name Jahmelia. I'll just call you Judy."

"I don't know anything about the organization level, as I do not know what kind of an impact a top-down approach in this regard can have on a person's beliefs. I do believe, however, that on a personal level it would be nice if everyone chose to pursue empathy, love and respect for others. Diversity and inclusion mean including everyone, in my opinion, even the people who we disagree with. I think that this should always be the message. It should extend across all races, religions, ethnicities, sexualities, etc., where no one group is favored or treated differently from the other."

—Anonymous

ACTION ITEMS

❏ Measure your demographics if you haven't already done so, and compare them to the demographics of your city, region or state. Can you do better?

❏ Review your policies, practices and procedures (the talent life cycle in particular) with a diversity frame of mind, and change what needs to be changed.

❏ Develop DEI strategies based on your measurements and then reassess after the strategies have been implemented.

❏ Educate leadership about the myths related to race and ethnicity. Hold leadership accountable.

CHAPTER 6

Are People of All Sexual Orientations Welcome Here?

Equality means more than passing laws. The struggle is really won in the hearts and minds of the community, where it really counts.

—BARBARA GITTINGS

Sexual Orientation versus Sexual Preference

Many people refer to lesbian, gay, and bisexual individuals as having a sexual preference rather than—more accurately—having a sexual orientation. It is not a preference—it is not chosen. It is an orientation.

This should be a settled issue, although it is not settled in some circles.

A Swedish study, published in the *Proceedings of the National Academy of Sciences* journal in 2004, compared the size of the brain halves in ninety adults. Gay men and heterosexual women had halves of a similar size, while the right side was bigger in lesbian women and heterosexual men.

Dr. Qazi Rahman, a lecturer in cognitive biology at Queen Mary University of London, said that he believed that these brain differences were created in early fetal development. "As far as I'm concerned there is no argument anymore—if you are gay, you are born gay," he said. "In other words, the brain network [amygdala] which determines

143

POWERING INCLUSIVE CULTURES

what sexual orientation 'orients' towards is similar between gay men and straight women, and between gay women and straight men. This makes sense given that gay men have a sexual preference which is like that of women in general, that is, preferring men, and vice versa for lesbian women."

My highly unscientific anecdotal information confirms this. The gay people I know have all known they were gay since puberty or earlier. It is not their "preference" that tells them they are gay, lesbian, bisexual or another orientation. It is simply the way they are.

In 2014, a study published in the National Library of Medicine looked at research showing that sexual orientation has a genetic component. "These studies show that sexual orientation is more concordant in monozygotic twins than in dizygotic ones and that male sexual orientation is linked to several regions of the genome." The study also looked at "women with congenital adrenal hyperplasia (CAH). These women were exposed to high levels of testosterone in utero and have much higher rates of non-heterosexual orientation compared to non-CAH women." So this research furthers the 2004 study showing that there are biological differences in homosexual versus heterosexual individuals.

. . . .

"Diversity is intended to mean diversity of opinion and background and should never be taken to mean diversity of sex, age, race, religion or sexual orientation, as those are irrelevant factors."

—Anonymous

. . . .

CASE STUDY: Preston Mitchum

I am a Black, gay and queer man from the Midwest. I have experienced discrimination based on my race, sexual orientation and class more times than imaginable. Because of what it means to be intersectional—that is, multiple marginalized identities existing at once—it is nearly impossible to determine whether I am experiencing discrimination and mistreatment on the basis of me being unapologetically Black or queer; and many times, both. In an ever-expanding and gentrifying Washington, DC, where I now reside, it's commonplace to be followed by law enforcement and be watched as I'm entering more expensive stores. While browsing in Georgetown, a majority-white area, I was once told to leave a store because I "was taking too long looking" just to be mocked by other staff. Not only was I in this particular store for less than ten minutes, but I was also certainly not the only one. I was profiled, targeted and belittled because of where I was and who I was perceived to be. No one defended me, no one made me feel human; and these are not isolated incidences. Every day, LGBTQ People of Color wake up understanding that we can be targeted at the intersection of our identities, and it is a perpetual process of healing and understanding.

Sexual Orientation Terms

To further your understanding about sexual orientation, here are several common terms and definitions provided by the Human Rights Campaign.

- **Ally** | A term used to describe someone who is actively supportive of LGBTQ+ people. It encompasses straight and cisgender allies, as well as those within the LGBTQ+ community who support each other (e.g., a lesbian who is an ally to the bisexual community).

- **Asexual** | Often called "ace" for short, asexual refers to a complete or partial lack of sexual attraction or lack of interest in sexual activity with others. Asexuality exists on a spectrum, and asexual people may experience no, little or conditional sexual attraction.

- **Bisexual** | A person emotionally, romantically or sexually attracted to more than one sex, gender or gender identity, though not necessarily simultaneously, in the same way or to the same degree. Sometimes used interchangeably with *pansexual.*

- **Cisgender** | A term used to describe a person whose gender identity aligns with that typically associated with the sex assigned to them at birth.

- **Coming Out** | The process in which a person first acknowledges, accepts and appreciates their sexual orientation or gender identity and begins to share that with others.

- **Gay** | A person who is emotionally, romantically or sexually attracted to members of the same gender. Men, women and nonbinary people may use this term to describe themselves.

- **Genderqueer** | Genderqueer people typically reject notions of static categories of gender and embrace a fluidity of gender identity and often, though not always, sexual orientation. People who identify as "genderqueer" may see themselves as being both male and female, neither male nor female or as falling completely outside these categories.

- **Homophobia** | The fear and hatred of or discomfort with people who are attracted to members of the same sex.

- **Lesbian** | A woman who is emotionally, romantically or sexually attracted to other women. Women and nonbinary people may use this term to describe themselves.

- **LGBTQ+** | An acronym for "lesbian, gay, bisexual, transgender and queer" with a "+" sign to recognize the limitless sexual orientations and gender identities used by members of our community.

- **Outing** | Exposing someone's lesbian, gay, bisexual, transgender or gender nonbinary identity to others without their permission. Outing someone can have serious repercussions on employment, economic stability, personal safety or religious or family situations.

- **Pansexual** | Describes someone who has the potential for emotional, romantic or sexual attraction to people of any gender, though not necessarily simultaneously, in the same way or to the same degree. Sometimes used interchangeably with *bisexual*.

- **Queer** | A term people often use to express a spectrum of identities and orientations that are counter to the mainstream. Queer is often used as a catch-all to include many people, including those who do not identify as exclusively straight and/or folks who have nonbinary or gender-expansive identities. This term was previously used as a slur but has been reclaimed by many parts of the LGBTQ+ movement.

- **Questioning** | A term used to describe people who are in the process of exploring their sexual orientation or gender identity.

- **Sexual orientation** | An innate or immutable and enduring emotional, romantic or sexual attraction to other people. Note: an individual's sexual orientation is independent of their gender identity.

- **Transgender** | An umbrella term for people whose gender identity and/or expression is different from cultural expectations based on the sex they were assigned at birth. Being transgender does not imply any specific sexual orientation. Therefore, transgender people may identify as straight, gay, lesbian, bisexual, etc.

As we mentioned in chapter 4, the *T* for *transgender* is a gender identity, not a sexual orientation. However, in terms of human rights advocacy, people who are transgender find commonality with the queer community. Their legal rights and fight against discrimination often coincide.

"I was once out with a level 6 employee who imitated one of our openly homosexual employees in a pretty nonflattering way. Not knowing the manager well, it didn't make a good impression. While s/he 'meant no harm,' the encounter showed me how that leader did not recognize that this could be offensive even if the person s/he was talking about was not in the room. So, more training regarding identifying our internal biases would be good. Specifically teaching us that we all have biases."

—Anonymous

As with gender and race, there is a continuum—or range—of sexual orientation. The percentages given in the following graphic are from the Gallup organization.

Continuum of Sexual Orientation

Sexual orientation per 100

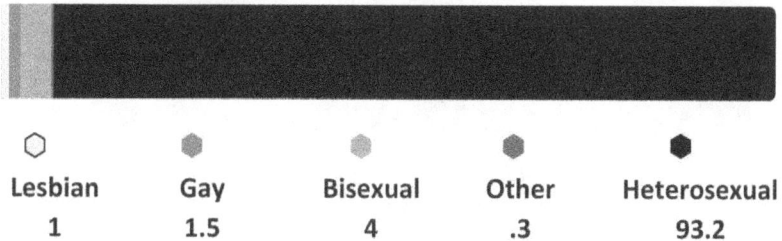

Lesbian	Gay	Bisexual	Other	Heterosexual
1	1.5	4	.3	93.2

LEARNING ACTIVITY

How Much Do You Know? (Answers in Appendix)

Mix and match. Pen or pencil. Right or wrong.

One in eight lesbian, gay and bi people (12 percent) wouldn't feel confident reporting any homophobic or biphobic bullying to their employer. ____ percent of trans people wouldn't report transphobic bullying in the workplace.

42

Without diverse leadership, those who identify as LGBTQ are ____ percent less likely than straight white men to win endorsement for their ideas.

54

Among LGBTQ+ people, ____ percent in these communities reported having been discriminated against because of their sexual orientation, and 16 percent reported that they had lost their job because of it.

21

Roughly ____ percent of gay men aged twenty-five or older in the US hold a bachelor's degree, according to new research published in the *American Sociological Review*, far higher than the national average of 36 percent.

21

____ percent of LGBTQ adults identify as bisexual. About a quarter (24.5 percent) say they are gay, with 11.7 percent identifying as lesbian and 11.3 percent as transgender.

52

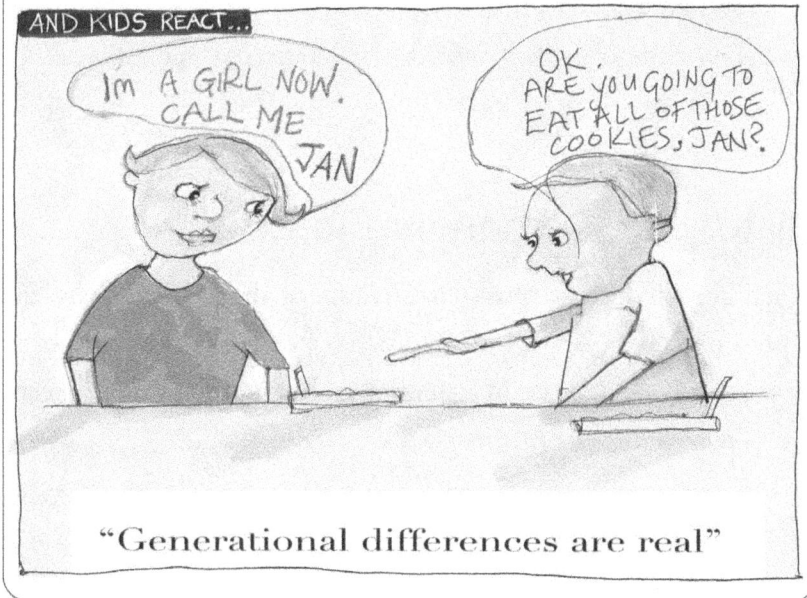

CASE STUDY: Naomi Washington Leapheart

This past June, my wife, Kentina, and I consecrated our legal marriage with a sacred wedding ceremony in the presence of our loved ones on a beach in Cape May, New Jersey. Three months later, we're still basking in the joy of that day. Our joy is sweeter because, in many ways, it is our resistance—not everyone was supportive of our union. In fact, we still ache as we remember that in January, a prospective wedding planner we considered hiring told us she couldn't work with us because she believes in the biblical definition of marriage, which, to her, made ours illegitimate. Kentina and I are Christian ministers. Our faith is precisely what animates our love and the decision we made to make a spiritual commitment to each other and to our communities. Yes, we are grateful that we could be legally married in any state in the country. Yet the rejection we experienced during one of the happiest seasons of our lives starkly reminded us that there is still so much more work to be done.

History Is a Demanding Teacher

Much like the history of systemic racism in the United States, the history of LGBTQ rights in the US has frequently been two steps forward and one step back. Depending on how old you are, the recent events may be in your memory bank.

US History of LGBTQ Rights

- 1691—Virginia passes the first antimiscegenation law, forbidding marriage between whites and Black people or whites and Native Americans (overturned in 1967 in *Loving v. Virginia*).

- 1779—Thomas Jefferson proposes Virginia law to make sodomy punishable by mutilation rather than death. It is rejected by the Virginia legislature.

- 1857–1861—James Buchanan is elected president. A lifelong bachelor, Buchanan had a long-term relationship with William Rufus King, who served as vice president under Franklin Pierce. The two men lived together from 1840–1853 until King's death. Some historians suggest Buchanan, by today's terms, was gay.

- 1896—*Plessy v. Ferguson*, by a vote of 7–1, declares racial segregation legal and is not an infringement on the equal protection clauses of the Fourteenth Amendment.

- 1933–1945—Nearly one hundred thousand German homosexual men are rounded up and placed in concentration camps along with Jewish people. They are designated by a pink triangle on their clothing.

- 1950—US Congress issues the report entitled "Employment of Homosexuals and Other Sex Perverts in Government," which is distributed to members of Congress after the federal government had covertly investigated employees' sexual orientation. The report states that since homosexuality is a mental illness, homosexuals "constitute security risks" to the nation.

- 1952—The American Psychiatric Association's diagnostic manual lists homosexuality as a sociopathic personality disturbance that could be treated. US Congress passes the Immigration Act barring "aliens afflicted with a psychopathic personality, epilepsy or mental defect." Congress makes clear that this was meant to exclude "homosexuals and sex perverts."

- 1969—Stonewall riots on June 28, also called the Stonewall uprising, begin when New York City police raid the Stonewall

Inn, a gay club located in Greenwich Village in New York City. The rough handling of the patrons is widely recognized as the beginning of the gay rights movement. The Gay Liberation Front organization forms in New York.

- 1973—The American Psychiatric Association changes the classification of homosexuality as a mental disorder. The APA finds that "the latest and best scientific evidence shows that sexual orientation and expressions of gender identity occur naturally ... and that in short, there is no scientific evidence that sexual orientation, be it heterosexual, homosexual or otherwise, is a freewill choice."

- 1978 (June 25)—In San Francisco, the rainbow flag is first flown during the Gay Freedom Day Parade; the flag becomes a symbol of gay and lesbian pride. (Nov. 27)—San Francisco supervisor Harvey Milk, who was openly gay, is assassinated along with Mayor George Moscone.

- 1981 (June 5)—AIDS epidemic begins. The US Centers for Disease Control and Prevention reports the first cases of a rare lung disease, which is named AIDS the following year. A total of 583,298 US men, women and children die from AIDS through 2007.

- 1993—The US Congress passes, and President Bill Clinton signs, "Don't Ask, Don't Tell," which allows gay and lesbian people to serve in the military. They would not be asked their sexual orientation during enlistment screening.

- 1998—Matthew Shepard, a twenty-one-year-old student at the University of Wyoming, is brutally attacked; tied to a fence in a field outside of Laramie, Wyoming; and left to die because he was gay. He dies from his wounds several days later. This results in a federal law passed ten years later in 2009 called the Hate Crimes Prevention Act, a federal law protecting against crimes of bias directed at lesbian, gay, bisexual or transgender people.

- 2003—*Lawrence v. Texas*, a Kansas law criminalizing gay or lesbian sex, is ruled unconstitutional.

- 2008—Proposition 8 passes with a 52 percent yes vote in California, declaring that marriage is between a man and a woman.

- 2013—*United States v. Windsor* / Repeal of the Defense of Marriage Act—DOMA: A vote of 5–4 rules that defining marriage as only between a man and a woman is unconstitutional under the Fifth Amendment guarantee of equal protection.

- 2015—*Obergefell v. Hodges*: The Supreme Court votes that the fundamental right to marry is guaranteed to same-sex couples by both the Due Process Clause and the Equal Protection Clause of the Fourteenth Amendment of the US Constitution. This decision mandates that states must allow same-sex couples to legally marry.

- 2016 (June 12)—The homophobic massacre at Pulse, a nightclub in Orlando, Florida, steals the lives of forty-two men, mostly gay and Latino, and seven women.

- 2022—*Roe v. Wade* is overturned by the US Supreme Court. *Roe v. Wade* used the same Fourteenth Amendment rationalizations as those used in *Obergefell v. Hodges*. As of this writing, many in the LGBTQ world are fearful that the right to marry and other rights based on the Fourteenth Amendment may be rolled back.

Homosexuality Is Against My Religion

In your organization there is probably at least one person who identifies with the subtitle above. Below is a respectful way to handle it if you're in the position to have a conversation with the other person. We'll call this person Pat.

Pat: My religion doesn't support the acceptance of gay people.

You: I hear what you're saying. Would you agree with me that there are probably people in our workforce who view themselves as gay (lesbian, LGBTQ, etc.)?

Pat: Yes.

You: Would you agree that in our workplace we always need the best talent all the time?

Pat: Yes.

You: And you want them to stay?

Pat: Yes.

You: There isn't a need for you to change your faith, but in the workplace, isn't there a need for every person to be respectful of each other?

Pat: Yes.

You: So what is it that bothers you?

Pat: It's about my faith.

> *You: In the workplace, day to day, what is it about your faith that bothers you about the gay community?*

> *Pat: I don't want anybody hitting on me or making advances because I'm straight.*

> *You: (optional) I always find it fascinating that straight people think gay people are going to waste their time hitting on straight people.*

> *Pat: (laughs)*

> *You: Would you agree that in the workplace that if someone is hitting on you or making advances, that it is inappropriate behavior? Period. For anyone.*

> *Pat: Yes.*

> *You: So what we need to do is separate inappropriate behavior from sexual orientation. They're two very different things. Let's focus on any inappropriate behavior.*

A conversation like this can help bridge the gap between someone resisting discussions or information about the LGBTQ community because of faith—and switching the conversation to behavior and respect, where it more properly belongs.

"Over the past few years, several people were using logos in their signature that had been edited to reflect holidays (Halloween, Christmas, Spring, Valentine's Day, etc.). Nothing was ever said until last June when several LGBTQIA+ flag logos started circulating for Pride Month. Almost immediately an email went out stating that the use of any altered logos was not allowed. Which is fine, but why was nothing said prior to that? Some folks had been using themed logos for years. I am cis and hetero, but that really hurt."

—Anonymous

CASE STUDY: Sonja

I spoke with Sonja recently. Her story illustrates the complications of a binary definition of both gender and sexual orientation. I asked her about her story of coming out and working in the tech industry.

As a young boy, I didn't have a lot of macho energy as a role model. That was OK until puberty, where I was having a hard time. I was confused and got my information from the internet—which is littered with porn. I was also a child of faith and was in a Christian rock band. Still confused, I talked to youth leadership in my Lutheran church. I was told "it's ok to be gay—just don't do anything about it." I gave my virginity to a guy and then was serial heteronormative for a while.

Heteronormative is when someone has a world view that heterosexuality is the normal or preferred sexual orientation. During this time Sonja was still presenting to others as a man and at the age of twenty-four married a woman. It ended in divorce.

I was working at an interactive design and technology agency. Their digital solutions transform the way busi-nesses around the globe communicate, sell and grow. My boss, the CEO, was out and proud. Her staff meetings were like going to church. The company had a culture of "There's rules—just check yourself before you go past them." I came out as transgender to them, and slowly things began to change. They pulled me from any public-facing roles in 2015. Then they took me out of the sales pipeline. The writing was on the wall, and I eventually left the organiza-tion, although the CEO didn't want me to go.

Her second marriage was as a transgender woman. Sonja worked as a freelancer for a while and then found a position with her current employer.

My current employer is a custom software development company with deep entrepreneurial experience that helps nontechnical founders build tech companies that succeed. I started out as a senior quality engineer, and I'm now the director of engineering. My boss is a serial entrepreneur who "walks the talk." The organization is an SBC—specific benefit corporation—which prioritizes social good as well as corporate success. Today I am bringing my "put-together self" to work every day, and I love it. I'm totally public facing now. I'm also in the sales pipeline. I don't have to use my "drive-through voice" (one pitched higher as a female) to work every day and am accepted as a transgender woman. I'm in a position of leader-ship, and I have several nonconforming employees reporting to me. This time the tech space has been great to me.

Just the Facts, Please

. . . .

"I know of at least two LGBTQIA+ folks who left due to not feeling comfortable being their authentic selves, and a third who opted for a fully remote position to avoid comments and criticism from coworkers. In my old department, I had been told to keep my more progressive views to myself so as not to offend anyone, while other more conservative members of the department were seemingly able to say what they wanted with no repercussions."

—Anonymous

. . . .

Travel is fatal to prejudice, bigotry and narrow-mindedness, and many of our people need it sorely on these accounts. Broad, wholesome, charitable views of men and things cannot be acquired by vegetating in one little corner of the earth all one's lifetime.

—MARK TWAIN

Let's travel through some data.

- 13,042,000 LGBTQ individuals in the US; 1.4 million of them are transgender.

- 700,000 cohabitating couples; 357,000 of them are married.

- 114,000 couples are raising children; 24 percent are raising adopted children.

- 20 percent of LGBTQ individuals earn less than $25,000 annually compared to 14 percent of straight individuals.

- 698,000 LGBTQ individuals have undergone conversion therapy; 350,000 of them underwent this therapy before they were eighteen. Conversion therapy is defined by WebMD as any emotional or physical therapy used to "cure" or "repair" a person's attraction to the same sex or their gender identity and expression. CEOs need to be aware of it because it doesn't work, and those who have been through it frequently have long-lasting issues such as depression.

- 15,500 transgender individuals are currently in the military; 134,000 veterans are transgender.

Earlier in chapter 2 we talked about how we are a combination of many qualities—some of which we had no choice over (skin color, eye color) or were influenced by our parents (geography, language, religion). It can be helpful for leaders to know how to accommodate an LGBTQ individual—should that individual choose to disclose their status.

Growing up can be a very difficult time for LGBTQ youth. Let's travel briefly down this road.

- Suicide is the second leading cause of death among young people aged ten to twenty-four; LGBTQ youth are more than four times as likely to attempt suicide than their peers.

- The Trevor Project estimates that more than 1.8 million LGBTQ youth (13–24) seriously consider suicide each year in the US—and at least one attempts suicide every forty-five seconds.

- 45 percent of LGBTQ youth seriously considered attempting suicide in 2021, including more than half of transgender and nonbinary youth.

- LGBTQ youth who reported undergoing conversion therapy were more than twice as likely to report having attempted suicide and more than 2.5 times as likely to report multiple suicide attempts in the past year.

Let's travel a bit further, a detour into the region of hate crimes.

- 2018—hate crimes against gender identity (nonbinary, third gender) was 2.2 percent of all hate crimes

- 2019—hate crimes against gender identity (nonbinary, third gender) grew to 2.7 percent of all hate crimes

- 2020—hate crimes based on sexual orientation represent 16.7 percent of hate crimes, the third-largest category after race and religion

- On a positive note, the Accelerating Acceptance study found that "non-LGBTQ Americans are becoming more understanding that the LGBTQ community is not just one homogeneous group, but rather a diverse community of various identities across gender and sexuality."

And last, let's end our travel with the LGBTQ scenarios in the workplace.

- LGBTQ women are more underrepresented than other women in America's largest corporations.

- LGBTQ women make up .06 percent of CEOs.

- LGBTQ men make up 2.9 percent of CEOs.

- Sixty-six percent of LGBTQ women of color have experienced being the "only" in meetings compared to 8 percent of straight white men.

- Twenty-six percent of LGBTQ women had obscene or sexually explicit comments directed at them compared to 10 percent of LGBTQ men and 5 percent of white men.

- Six in twenty LGBTQ men believe that their sexual orientation will negatively affect their career advancement at work.

. . . .

"I grew up in a loving and conservative Christian home where I was taught certain messages that I do not ascribe to (including that homosexuality is a sin and draws people away from being close to God). It was challenging to move away from some of these early teachings."

—Anonymous

. . . .

Based on the 2022 Annual Spectra Assessment Report, LGBTQ people in general scored lower in their perceptions of management's behavior. There are many categories in the graphic below. Note that men are the highest scoring group (19.25) with straight individuals (18.71), LGBTQ individuals (17.32) falling below that and nonbinary/third gender (15.95) at the very bottom.

The LGBTQ population also scored lower on their perceptions of their organization's policies, practices and procedures related to diversity and inclusion as well as their company's culture.

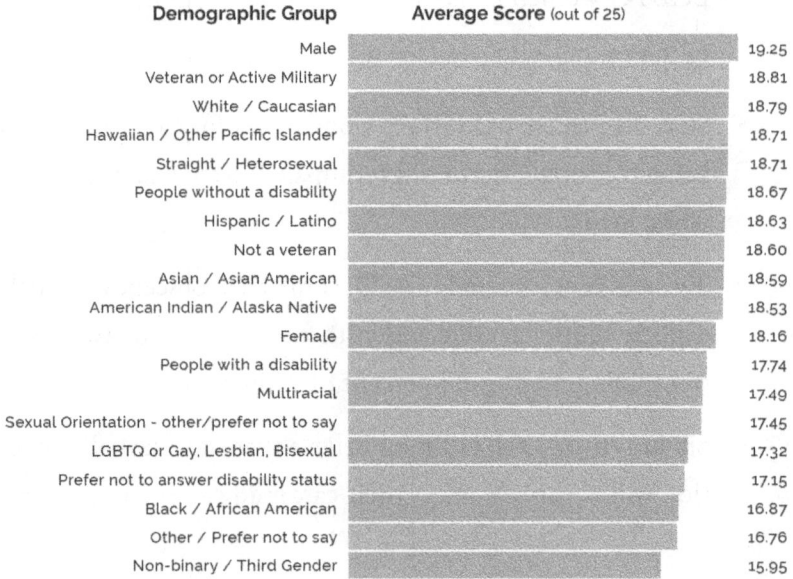

Demographic Group	Average Score (out of 25)	
Male		19.25
Veteran or Active Military		18.81
White / Caucasian		18.79
Hawaiian / Other Pacific Islander		18.71
Straight / Heterosexual		18.71
People without a disability		18.67
Hispanic / Latino		18.63
Not a veteran		18.60
Asian / Asian American		18.59
American Indian / Alaska Native		18.53
Female		18.16
People with a disability		17.74
Multiracial		17.49
Sexual Orientation - other/prefer not to say		17.45
LGBTQ or Gay, Lesbian, Bisexual		17.32
Prefer not to answer disability status		17.15
Black / African American		16.87
Other / Prefer not to say		16.76
Non-binary / Third Gender		15.95

. . . .

"I would hope that our organization needing to meet some quota of diversity doesn't overlook the best qualified individual for a position because he/she is a white heterosexual individual. I have witnessed instances where individuals have avoided termination or discipline because of their skin color or gender. I know the issues were never taken to HR but just handled by the department manager. Quite frankly I am tired of these topics and tired of feeling the need to frequently apologize for being a white heterosexual female. It appears that in today's culture I am valued less because I do not meet the diverse quota that needs to be met because of my ethnicity, sexual orientation or how I identify my gender."

—Anonymous

. . . .

Lead Like an Ally

Based on general population numbers, as a leader you're more likely to be an ally of those who are LGBTQ rather than to count yourself as one of their members. In our training, we give simple guidelines to what you can say if someone disparages an LGBTQ individual or makes a comment or action that is a subtle act of exclusion (SAE).

To an LGBTQ individual:

- **"I'll bet your house is gorgeous."**

- **"Your name tag should have glitter, don't you think?"**

- **"I'm assuming your children are adopted because you're ... you know ..."**

Subtle acts of exclusion are slightly different from microaggressions. A microaggression has the word *aggression* in it—which isn't the case in many instances. Someone could commit an SAE in a nonintentional way. Think of it more as uneducated rather than intentional.

LEARNING ACTIVITY

This may be an activity which you could make into a workplace poster.

What to Do When You're a Target of a Subtle Act of Exclusion

For example, "What do gay people think about that?" assumes that all people who are gay have the same opinion and that one can somehow speak for everyone.

- Remain calm and find a way to pause from assuming or reacting right away.

- Give the benefit of the doubt. Taking extreme stances as either a victim or a "tough" person can ultimately hurt you. Remember that people are often unaware of their offensive comment or action.

- Ask clarifying questions. You can ask, "Why are you surprised that I am articulate? Help me understand why you are surprised that I speak well" or "What do you mean, 'That is gay'?"

- Focus on the event, not the person. By directing the conversation to the behavior, event or comment you will decrease the likelihood of defensiveness.

What to Do When You're a Bystander Who Witnesses a Subtle Act of Exclusion

For example, "I wonder if she's the man or the woman in the relationship?" assumes that two genders are necessary to have a relationship.

- Be an ally. It's important for allies to know that sometimes their voices can be heard even more powerfully than those of the people directly affected by an SAE.

- Speak for yourself. Don't try to speak on behalf of the person who has experienced the SAE since doing so can itself be a form of SAE.

What to Do When You've Committed a Subtle Act of Exclusion

For example, "Is it awkward bringing your partner as the plus-one at events?" assumes that having a same-sex partner is not normal.

- You are not a bad person. The first thing to remember is that committing an SAE is not indicative that we're bad people; it's more indicative of a society where certain stereotypes are engrained in our culture from the media, our families and our friends.

- Try not to be defensive. If someone else is accusing you of an SAE, take into consideration that the person may be nervous to share this info with you.

- Acknowledge the other person's hurt, apologize and reflect on where the SAE came from and how you can avoid similar mistakes in the future.

A DEI colleague of mine, Julie Kratz, wrote *Lead Like an Ally* which has several great ideas in it.

Test it. If someone doesn't want to meet with an LGBTQ person, try the "**flip it to test it**" technique. Ask them whether they would have the same concern if the individual were straight? If they say no (as they probably will), then use the conversation with Pat in this chapter to find out what is really bothering them. What is the real fear or concern?

Challenge bias. If someone in your organization asks *you* about the sexual orientation of another person, just say, "Did you ask them?" One shouldn't assume someone is gay, just as one shouldn't assume that they're not gay. If it has no immediate bearing on your work, it is none of your business. The absolute *worst* thing you can do is to out somebody who prefers to keep their sexual orientation private.

Create an ERG. You can ask Human Resources to help you set this up, although if you're a leader, you should make everyone aware that it has your full support. You can act as the sponsor and **give them a budget**. The ERG is a safe place to share concerns, tell stories and create actions that can be implemented to increase diversity, equity and inclusion across the organization.

Partner with recruiting agencies that focus on diverse candidates, or deeply train the internal HR/recruiting folks on diversity hiring.

Pair with an organization that can provide diverse interns to use, which could turn into hires.

Measure the entire organization and then focus on diverse leadership as the first place to do your DEI work. Only by seeing People of Color or people that are different at the top will the entire organization begin to value the inclusion of the opinions and experiences of those unlike themselves. Make sure executive leadership is deeply taught and coached in DEI matters/concerns/biases and approaches to better the culture. Change comes from within, but it starts at the top. If the top leaders are not enacting all the things the employees are, then the whole DEI attempt is just lip service.

Offer robust selections of learning modules to include unconscious bias, systemic racism, white fragility, how to discuss race/

religion in the workplace, gender bias, sexual harassment or famous LGBTQ people in history, to name a few.

Offer an optional book club where a selected work is read and discussed in an open, inclusive way. Maybe pair the book club with a film screening of the same book. How are they different? Why are they different? Only by offering people the platform to talk about race/gender/cultural differences will people be open to having the conversations.

Explore ways to celebrate all cultures (difficult in work-from-home times, when nobody is in the office), honor and acknowledge holidays that not everyone celebrates, in addition to the obvious default white Anglo-Saxon Protestant ones like Christmas. How about a nod to Diwali? Or a learning module on "What is Ramadan"? Maybe LGBTQ Bingo!

ACTION ITEMS

- ❑ Did you measure? You must measure to know how your LGBTQ employees may have unique perceptions of your organization.

- ❑ Educate yourself.

- ❑ Remember that being gay is a sexual orientation—not a preference.

- ❑ Build trust with accountability for how LGBTQ employees are treated.

CHAPTER 7

Are You Providing Accommodations for People with a Disability?

Until the great mass of the people shall be filled with the sense of responsibility for each other's welfare, social justice can never be attained.

—HELEN KELLER

The Stigma Is Real

Social justice is a lofty goal—as is removing systemic racism from society and our organizations. That doesn't mean we shouldn't try. It's good for business and good for the world.

Those who are without a disability are not empowering those with disabilities. To make the systemic changes needed in organizations and culture in general, people with disabilities must have equal access to the *power* necessary to function fully as themselves.

Even though it is estimated that 30 percent of people in the workforce have a disability, many choose to keep their status confidential. An individual in a wheelchair or one who uses a cane to walk doesn't have the option of keeping their status private. Many others have the option not to disclose, and they use it.

Seventy-five percent of Disabilities Are Invisible

I recently began checking the box for "disability" because I'm being treated for depression. Without medication, I spiral into lethargy, darkness and relationship-shattering irritability. So I check the box. I take my pill.

A woman I know does not check the disability box and refuses to apply for Social Security Disability Insurance (SSDI). She has had type 1 diabetes since her twenties and has suffered many health challenges since then. One of the worst consequences is gastroparesis. It is a condition that makes her unable to digest food properly. Food digestion is a combination of enzymes in your gut microbiome and a squeezing motion made by your stomach to move the food through the digestive track. Gastroparesis means that her gastric system (gastro) is paralyzed (paresis). It doesn't squeeze. This results in two issues—often simultaneously—vomiting and diarrhea. There are currently a few FDA approved drugs (prescription only) that work to encourage the food to move.

She frequently misses events and had to quit her job because of frequent bathroom bouts—some of which last for days. And still she won't apply for SSDI payments because "That's for disabled people." She maintains this view even though she has paid into Social Security for her entire working life.

Diabetes on its own is one of several "manageable" diseases that can result in disability. Multiple sclerosis is another one. As is cancer. A person undergoing cancer treatment may need accommodations for a while—or for their lifetime.

Common types of mental and physical disabilities

PHYSICAL PROBLEM	EMOTIONAL/MENTAL PROBLEM
Asthma (or other breathing problems)	Age-related cognitive decline
Blindness (and partial blindness)	Any psychiatric condition
Deafness (and partial deafness)	Autism
Diabetes	Depression
Dizziness / balance problems	Dyslexia
Epilepsy	Bipolar disorder
General hearing difficulty	Emotional overwhelm
Mobility problems	Panic attacks
Neurological problems	Posttraumatic stress disorder (PTSD)
Paralysis	Separation anxiety
Physical weakness	Social phobia
Speech problems	Stress problems
Seizures	

Self-identification of a visible or invisible disability remains an issue. The stigma is real.

LEARNING ACTIVITY

How Much Do You Know? (Answers in Appendix)

When we think of disability, we often think of a person in a wheelchair or an individual who is blind. Ability and disability go far beyond that.

_____ percent of adults in the US have some type of disability. The percentage of people living with disabilities is highest in the South.

90

The 2021 jobless rate for those with a disability was about twice as high as the rate for those without a disability. In 2021, _____ percent of workers with a disability were employed part time, compared with 16 percent for those with no disability.

30

The Department of Labor found that employers who supported those with disabilities saw a _____ percent increase in employee retention. (Offering reasonable accommodations is often significantly less costly than firing workers.)

26

Companies that prioritized the inclusion of individuals with disabilities were four times more likely to outperform their competitors in shareholder returns and have, on average 28 percent higher revenue, double the net income and _____ percent higher profit margins.

29

_____ percent of accommodations cost absolutely nothing to make, while the rest typically cost only five hundred dollars per employee with a disability.

59

Begin with Measurement

Continuum of Disability

Ability in millions

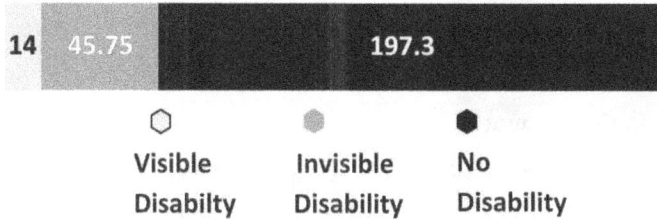

14	45.75	197.3

○	◉	⬢
Visible Disabilty	**Invisible Disability**	**No Disability**

The above chart includes all adults eighteen years or older and those who may have retired.

In Spectra Diversity's assessment, we track six demographics as a minimum:

1. Race/ethnicity (may select more than one)

2. Gender identity

3. Ability/disability

4. Sexual orientation

5. Age

6. Veteran status

In the thousands of assessments that we've done at Spectra Diversity, we have *never* had an assessment show 30 percent of the organization's populace to be mentally or physically disabled. The closest we've come at self-identification is 3 percent.

According to a report published by Accenture, in partnership with Disability:IN and the American Association of People with Disabilities (AAPD), there are 15.1 million people of working age living with disabilities in the US. "The research suggests that if companies embrace disability inclusion, they will gain access to a new talent pool of more than 10.7 million people." In 2022, with unemployment at a low of 3.6 percent, making minor accommodations for people with a disability—and making your accommodations public when you recruit—could give you a strategic advantage and put this underutilized population to work.

The US Office of Disability Employment Policy categorizes persons with disabilities as the third-largest market segment in the US, after Hispanic and Black people. The discretionary income for working-age persons with disabilities is $21 billion—greater than that of the Black and Hispanic segments combined.

What Was That I Heard?

In the previous chapter, we learned the term *subtle acts of exclusion* as a replacement for *microaggressions*. The list of subtle acts of exclusion and hurtful comments aimed (innocently) at people with disabilities is long. These subtle acts of inclusion are adapted from *Subtle Acts of Exclusion: How to Understand, Identify, and Stop Microaggressions*, by Tiffany Jana and Michael Baran of Inquest Consulting.

Eight Types of Subtle Acts of Exclusion That Are Commonly Present

1. You don't belong—"I saw some other [Asians, Hispanics, Blacks] going to lunch. They went that way." (Assuming your automatic connection when there might not be one.)

2. You are invisible—"You must be new here." (You've been there for two years.)

3. You are a threat—Moving away when you come near: crossing the street, for example, or hearing the door lock click as a car drives past you.

4. You are not an individual—"Tell me what your people think about [Black Lives Matter, voting rights, any controversial topic]." (Implying that your group is a monolith.)

5. You are inadequate—"I assume you're being given the extra help you need."

6. You are a curiosity—"Can I touch your hair? Your dreadlocks are amazing."

7. You are not normal—"It must be hard knowing you can never have a biological child." (To gay or lesbian people, for example.)

8. You are a burden—"You must get tired of everyone always having to open doors for you." (To a person in a wheelchair or using a walker.)

Below are some absolutes for your leadership team (and employees) when speaking with individuals with a disability. Keep in mind that speaking respectfully should always occur because 75 percent of individuals with disabilities have invisible disabilities. You could be speaking about disabilities to an individual with a disability without knowing it.

Word Order Matters

Identify the individual first—and then any disability. Say "a man who is visually impaired/blind" rather than "a blind man" or "woman in a wheelchair" rather than "a handicapped woman." The person first and then the descriptive language.

APPROPRIATE LANGUAGE	INAPPROPRIATE LANGUAGE
People with disabilities/ staff or students with disabilities	The disabled/handicapped/ physically challenged/ incapacitated
People who are blind / people with visual impairment	The blind / visually impaired
People who are deaf / people who are hard of hearing	The deaf / hearing impaired
Person with epilepsy	Epileptic
Person who uses a wheelchair or wheelchair user	Wheelchair bound / confined to a wheelchair
Person with intellectual disabilities / person with learning difficulties	Mentally handicapped / retarded
Person living with AIDS	Victim of AIDS / AIDS sufferer
A person with cerebral palsy	Spastic
People without a disability	Normal / able bodied

Nothing about Us without Us

I've learned that many of the terms used for people with a disability were invented by people without disabilities.

- *Do not* say "handicapped," "special needs," "differently abled" or "handicapable."

- *Do not* say "I don't see you as disabled," which is denying the individual a portion of their identity.

- *Do* ask how a person would like to be defined (assuming you need to identify them for some reason). Just as you should ask a Black person if they identify as Black versus African American, do the same for any individual with a disability.

Know the Law

The Americans with Disabilities Act (ADA) requires covered employers to provide effective, reasonable accommodations for employees with disabilities. To help determine effective accommodations, the Equal Employment Opportunity Commission (EEOC), recommends that employers use an "interactive process," which simply means that employers and employees with disabilities who request accommodations work together to come up with accommodations. To have a disability under the ADA, an individual must have an impairment that substantially limits one or more major life activities. Changes in the interpretation of the definition of the term *disability* resulting from enactment of the ADA Amendments Act (ADAAA) make it easier for employees who have pregnancy-related impairments to demonstrate that they have disabilities for which they may be entitled to reasonable accommodation.

Accommodations Can Benefit Everyone

Several accommodations made because of the ADA are benefiting many individuals beyond those for whom it was originally intended.

- Sidewalk curb ramps—originally made to accommodate wheelchairs but are used by baby strollers, bicyclists and those with vision or other mobility problems.

- Automatic door openers—once again created for wheelchairs, these are used by people carrying boxes or groceries. Have you ever bumped your hip against an automatic door opener as a matter of convenience? I certainly have.

- Stair ramps—not only used for wheelchairs but also for people with bad knees and others for whom stairs are difficult.

- Handicapped parking—can be a temporary accommodation to someone with a sprained ankle or broken leg.

- Nursing rooms—created for new mothers to either nurse or pump breast milk in privacy and can also be a refuge for women with menstrual cramps or other temporary issues.

- Flexible scheduling—accommodates those with anxiety, PTSD and other similar conditions and can also be used to work around rush hour or transportation issues for in-office workers.

- Additional time to complete written tasks—can benefit those who have dyslexia as well as those for whom English is a second language and are busy translating in their heads.

"I personally reached out to HR to tell them I was going on antidepressants and that I wanted to know if there would be anything I would have to do if I found that depression was impacting my job. I got *no* response. Not even a "Thanks for letting us know." Why wouldn't there be some protocol to at least send our insurance providers' number to help under-stand our mental health benefits? Listen, I am not jaded, nor am I surprised, but I think this is a valid example of how pervasive an issue our company can have to being inclusive."

—Anonymous

But the Cost!

Remember the "flip it to test it" advice from the previous chapter? Let's try that here. Instead of thinking about the cost of accommodating people with disabilities, think about the money you are leaving on the table if you do *not* include people with disabilities in your talent pool and your consumer/customer market.

- Champion organizations (those with diversity inclusive policies, practices and procedures) were twice as likely as others to have higher total shareholder returns than those of their peer group.

- Companies that have improved their inclusion of persons with disabilities over time were four times more likely than others to have total shareholder returns that outperform those of their peer group.

- The Job Accommodation Network, a service from the US Department of Labor's Office of Disability Employment Policy, reported that 59 percent of accommodations cost absolutely nothing to make, while the rest typically cost only five hundred dollars per employee with a disability.

CASE STUDY: Greg Jenkins

Greg is a disabled veteran. People who have not been in the military may not know how the military treats disabilities as percentages. Someone who is a double amputee, for example, would be 100 percent disability. My father is 80 percent disabled because of loss of hearing. Greg is a 40 percent disability veteran, which means he has all his fingers and toes but that the wear and tear on his body after twenty-nine years in the military has taken a toll. In Greg's words,

> disability is an equal opportunity employer. I think there's north of fifty-five million Americans right now, this minute, that are disabled people. If disability was a protected category, it would be the largest minority group in the US. And the thing about disability is that it does not discriminate: rich, poor, white, Black, brown, Asian, gay, straight, pray, don't pray. You can be in a car accident, fall off a ladder, contract some kind of debilitating, lifelong illness, and you're in that group. You're in the club.
>
> And that population of people with a disability is woefully underemployed even when they're able to work! They

have skill sets; they've got training. That's the whole reason why we have the ADA, Americans with Disabilities Act, which I think George H. W. Bush signed. And the whole idea was that one of the many things about the ADA was to provide reasonable accommodation so that you could hire somebody in your business that could come in and be an employee. And "reasonable" might mean installing a ramp on a set of stairs so the wheelchair could go up, as an example, or it's an adjustable, higher desk so a wheelchair could fit under it, again as another example. Or software for people that have limited vision abilities. So there are legitimate, very reasonable accommodations that can be made.

I remember reading not too long ago where persons with disability have higher retention rates, in many cases over able-body people. Once they get in a position, they really hang on. They show up because they understand how difficult it may be to get another job. So, they really want to perform, and many of them do very well.

Greg shared with me a story like my friend who doesn't want to collect Social Security Disability Insurance payments.

I have a friend of mine, a colleague, who has been blind since birth, and even he said "I didn't want to be considered a disabled person even though I am completely blind." I don't think that's unusual.

The stigma is real.

183

I'm not saying that people with disabilities are damaged goods, but they can be perceived as that when an employer is hiring. Because we all have biases and stereotypes and then when we see a wheelchair or disabled person and think—I don't know if they're really going to be able to work here when they may be the best person to work here. What's the requirements of the job? What does that look like? But perceptions and biases are really powerful, and we need to slow down enough to gather information about that person. They are a viable candidate. Not only are they a viable candidate, but they also made it into the final interview cycle. And maybe they get the job. And I think that's where the real challenge shows up for employers when they think "talent[ed] candidate," they think, "That's going to be a very healthy, well-educated, very motivated, able-bodied human being." And that can be that descriptor of a person, but they can also be well educated, motivated, paraplegic and great for the job.

The Benefits of Neurodiversity

As with many types of diversity, hiring neurodiverse employees can provide certain advantages while also requiring occasional accommodations. Those who are neurodiverse may or may not be considered disabled. In the Spectra Assessment, employees are allowed to self-identify, so some may select that they have a mental disability while others do not select this option.

- People with Attention Deficit Hyperactivity Disorder (ADHD) have high spontaneity levels, courage and empathy.

They can hyperfocus on tasks. If you are a manager with an ADHD employee, you will seldom be at a loss for wondering about their opinions.

- People with autism can pay attention to complex details, have good memories and, in some instances, have highly developed specific skills, such as computer programming.

- People with dyslexia can be better at visual information processing and would be a good fit for engineering or computer graphics.

Types of Neurodiversity

There are several forms of neurodiversity, which can present both challenges and opportunities for the individual and the employer. *Neurodiversity* refers to the idea that certain brain conditions are not developmental disorders but are in fact normal variations in the brain. So, like melanin in the skin varies between individuals, there is a range of brain functions which can fall under the umbrella of "normal." Below are common types of neurodiversity in the workplace.

- **ADHD** is a condition characterized by inattention, distraction and disorganization. These people can be impulsive. More males than females present with ADHD, and it frequently lessens after childhood. Richard Branson is a famous example.

- **Autism** is a spectrum of conditions which can be mild or severe. One of the milder forms is Asperger's syndrome. Those with Asperger's may be very intelligent and able to handle their daily life but may lack social skills. Famous individuals with Asperger's include Dan Akroyd, Sir Anthony Hopkins, and Andy Warhol. A more severe form of autism is pervasive developmental disorder, not otherwise specified (PDD-NOS). According to autismspeaks.org, 1 in 27 boys are identified with autism compared to 1 in 116 girls. All ethnicities are represented.

- **Dyslexia** is a learning disability that makes it difficult to read, write and spell despite normal intelligence and adequate instruction. The brain does not process the written word as most brains do, and so people with this condition must learn in other ways. Albert Einstein, Bill Gates, Henry Ford and Richard Branson had/have this condition.

- **Dyspraxia** is a brain-based motor disorder. It affects fine and gross motor skills, motor planning and coordination. Daniel Radcliff (of *Harry Potter* fame) has dyspraxia and has trouble with simple coordination activities such as tying his shoelaces. His mother had him audition for a play to help improve his self-esteem. It seemed to work out for him! According to Healthline, dyspraxia is characterized by

  - a short attention span for tasks that are difficult,

  - trouble following or remembering instructions,

  - a lack of organizational skills,

  - difficulty learning new skills,

  - low self-esteem,

  - immature behavior and

  - trouble making friends.

"As we have focused on Black Lives Matter since the summer of 2020, looking towards new ways to foster diversity and inclusion around other racial differences, gender identity and disability would be good next steps."

—Anonymous

Leadership Strategies

You do not need to start this on your own and build a disability inclusion policy from scratch. Others have built it already and you can start with their procedures and modify to fit your organization.

Build on the Work of Others

The Job Accommodation Network (JAN) has an entire section of free templates for you to use. Their resources include the following:

- Examples of Accommodation Policy and Processes
- Accommodation Flowchart
- Examples of Training
- Example Handbook for Non-Visible Disabilities
- Sample Forms
- Onboarding Checklist
- ADA Request Form
- Accommodation Request Form
- Accommodation Assessment Form
- Return to Work Functional Assessment Form

- Accommodation Tracking Spreadsheet Sample
- Telework Policies

Talent Pipeline Review

Examine your talent pipeline with disabilities in mind—beginning with your hiring process and moving to employee onboarding; performance reviews and promotions; and, finally, exit interviews.

- Are your website and job postings accessible to people who are blind or low vision? Add alt-text and image descriptions to visual content.

- Design internal and external content that meets digital accessibility standards.

- Make meetings and events (whether in person or virtual) accessible to all.

- Use the interviewing process to anticipate needs and discuss potential accommodations early on.

- Reach out to disability networks when conducting your talent search.

Neurocognitive Differences

If you're an employer interested in innovation or in creating a more diverse workforce to attract employees, welcoming people with neurocognitive differences may require a few adjustments in the workplace. Neurodiversity is the diversity of human brains and minds—the infinite variation in neurocognitive functioning within our species. A neurocognitive difference is not necessarily a disability.

- Those who are neurodiverse may be highly sensitive to stimuli. As a manager, it would be beneficial (for everyone, perhaps?) to pay attention to work-life balance and model good behavior. A neurodiverse person may benefit from alternative desk placement, the ability to work from home, specific job hours or other common workplace adjustments.

- Ask before assigning. By the time a neurodiverse person is an adult, they probably have a good idea of what they excel at and what is a challenge. When assigning projects—ask first. There may be something at which the employee with neurodiversity may excel—well beyond what others may achieve.

- Add training and education for leaders regarding how to manage a neurodiverse employee. Training is not the answer to every issue of course, but it's a good place to start.

Walk the Talk

Your organization can do more. Consider supporting groups like ADAPT (American Disabled for Attendant Programs Today). ADAPT fights for disability justice and strives to promote and embrace the differences among us, our similar struggles and our shared efforts to break free of those institutions that bind us physically, socially and mentally. One key initiative ADAPT is supporting is the Disability Integration Act (DIA). DIA is a civil right, bipartisan and bicameral legislation to address the fundamental issue that people who need long-term services and supports (LTSS) are forced into institutions and losing their basic civil rights.

Create a Group

Based on the previous chapters of this book, you may be considering the creation of employee resource groups. A disability ERG would be a great addition to your organization and would be a great way to identify additional accommodations to benefit those with disabilities—and perhaps become standard operating procedures for all.

ACTION ITEMS

❑ Measure the physical and mental disability among your employees. The objective of measuring is not simply to collect this data but to use it to make better decisions.

❑ Recruit with inclusion in mind. There are millions of individuals with disabilities in your potential talent pool, and one could be your next genius hire.

❑ Hire with accommodation in mind. Most accommodations don't cost anything other than your time to implement them.

CHAPTER 8

Are You Undervaluing Your Older and Younger Employees?

I will never be an old man. To me, old age
is always 15 years older than I am.

—FRANCIS BACON

Stereotypes Running Amok

If someone told a so-called joke using a racist stereotype or about an individual who is gay, lesbian or transgender, the negative reaction from those listening could be swift.

However, when someone tells a "joke" using a stereotype related to age, it may not have a negative reaction at all. "Hey boomer!" "Get off my lawn!" "You're too young to be my doctor!" "You can't teach an old dog new tricks." LOL—right? Wrong.

Workplace age discrimination is not a laughing matter. My own experience is just one anecdote, but it confirms the difficulties faced by those over a certain age.

Since 1985 I had been an independent contractor with long-term clients. I wasn't getting rich, but I paid my mortgage on time and had raised my children as a single mom for several years. I was in my fifties when the financial crisis of 2008 hit. The Great Recession had begun and led to some of the highest recorded rates of unemployment and home foreclosures in the US since the Great Depression. During that time, my clients disappeared en masse.

191

"Do the math, for your vet bills alone we can hire two pups."

They cut their sales and marketing and training budgets—where most of my work took place. They also kept more work in house rather than hiring outside contractors.

My income took a swift nosedive. I picked up a few new skills (building websites using WordPress and search engine optimization), continued to look for freelance work, and at the same time started applying for corporate jobs. The jobs I applied for were the same jobs I had been doing as a successful freelancer for decades.

I also went on unemployment. If you've never been on unemployment, you might be surprised to discover that, despite the enormous amount of paperwork you're expected to do, the resulting benefit might not even cover your mortgage. I dropped my health insurance coverage (with fingers crossed) and started withdrawing from my savings account to pay for utilities, gas and groceries. I continued looking for new freelance work at the same time I looked for full-time employment—which I had not had since 1985. Out of hundreds of applications and resumes sent out, I got *one* interview, and it was because of a referral.

Was I too experienced? Was my hourly rate too high? Did I have a typo on my résumé? Or was I simply beyond the "sell by" date? I'll never know.

Although age discrimination typically falls on the older end of the spectrum, those on the younger end of the spectrum can be subjected to denigrating comments as well. A book editor I know was promoted to acquisitions editor at age twenty-six. One of her authors asked bluntly, "Are you old enough to be my editor?" That wasn't the last time an author commented on her age, and it still happens in her thirties.

For reference, these are the birthdate ranges for the current working generations:

- Silent Generation (1928–1945)
- Baby boomer (1946–1964)
- Generation X (1965–1980)
- Millennial (1981–1996)
- Generation Z (1997–2012)

Continuum of Age

Age in millions

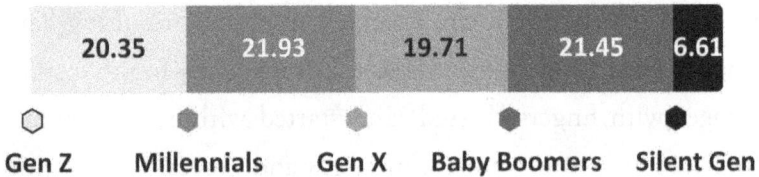

20.35	21.93	19.71	21.45	6.61
Gen Z	Millennials	Gen X	Baby Boomers	Silent Gen

The above chart is in millions. You can see that if you combine the younger generations (millennials and Gen Z) you have 42.28 million, and if you combine the two older generations (Gen X and baby boomers) you have 41.16 million. When you consider the workforce, this seemingly equal position isn't quite equal because the baby boomers are retiring. The actual workforce is becoming overwhelmingly younger. It's an echo of the baby boom.

Test Yourself

Implicit Association Test

Have you taken Harvard's Implicit Association Test? We mentioned it in chapter 3 to look at your biases related to race and gender. Another bias test you can take is related to age. I took the age IAT and am embarrassed to admit that it shows I have a slight age bias—toward old people and against young people.

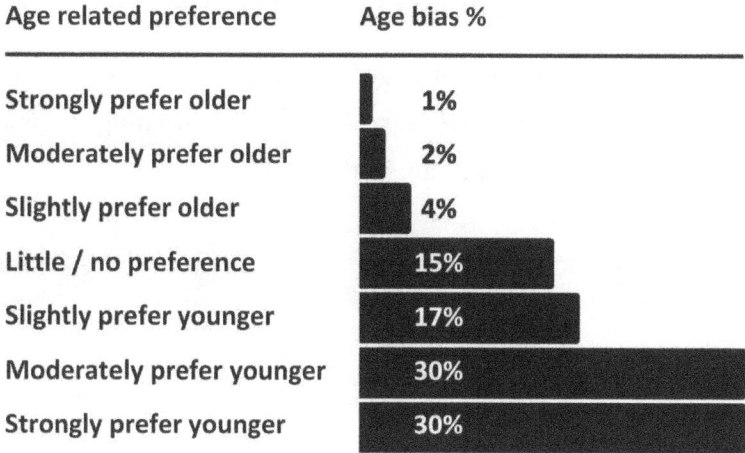

Age related preference	Age bias %
Strongly prefer older	1%
Moderately prefer older	2%
Slightly prefer older	4%
Little / no preference	15%
Slightly prefer younger	17%
Moderately prefer younger	30%
Strongly prefer younger	30%

My children are millennials who, according to a Bloomberg report of 2021, currently have $360 billion in disposable income, more than double what was estimated three years ago.

Because of my IAT age bias results, I am now constantly reminding myself that they might know what they're talking about. Imagine that?! My slight bias in favor of old people is in stark contrast to most people who take the IAT who prefer young people compared to old people. Above is a chart that shows the distribution summaries for nearly one million IAT scores for the age task. I am clearly an outlier (4 percent) for my results in the IAT age test.

LEARNING ACTIVITY

True/False Quiz about Aging

If you're a baby boomer, you may get 100 percent on this short quiz—because you're either sixty-five years old or fast approaching that magic age. The answers to this quiz are in the appendix.

AGING STATEMENT	TRUE	FALSE
1. It is possible to improve some of the memory loss often experienced by the elderly.		
2. The majority of older adults become senile or demented.		
3. Falling is one of the major causes of injury in older adults.		
4. Twenty-five percent of all persons over age sixty-five live in institutions.		
5. Depression is a serious problem for older adults.		
6. Personality changes with age.		
7. Stress in a caregiver's life is rarely a factor for triggering abuse of an older adult.		
8. Family members today do not provide as much care for their older relatives as they did in the past.		

How did you do? This short quiz, like the implicit association test, helps to reveal biases. When a bias is uncovered, it can be changed. It's a mindset difference.

The short quiz below is on the other end of the spectrum. If you're forty or older, you may lump millennials and Gen Z together. They have a very different set of preferences, however. For reference, millennials are those born 1981–1996 and Gen Z are those born after 1997. The answers to this quiz are in the appendix.

LEARNING ACTIVITY

True/False Quiz about Generation Z

GEN Z STATEMENT	TRUE	FALSE
Gen Z is the last generation to have a white majority.		
Gen Z is generally progressive and progovernment.		
Gen Z is more likely to be children of immigrants compared to millennials.		
Gen Z is on track to become the most educated generation yet.		
Gen Z is the first truly digital generation.		
Gen Z is more likely to have college-educated parents compared to millennials.		
Gen Z are less likely to be working during their teen years compared to previous generations.		
Gen Z agrees with millennials that climate change is due to human activity.		

Concerns for the Future

When we're thinking about putting the *power* into an inclusive culture, keep in mind that the generations working in your organization don't necessarily want or need the same things. They have different worries.

According to a study by Deloitte, Gen Zers (29 percent) and millennials (36 percent) selected cost of living (e.g., housing, transport, bills, etc.) as their greatest concern. In addition, 12 percent of Gen Zers and 11 percent of millennials selected political instability, war and conflicts between countries as their greatest concern. This last percentage would likely be higher if the research was conducted after the invasion of Ukraine.

- Almost half of Gen Zers (46 percent) and millennials (47 percent) live paycheck to paycheck and worry they won't be able to cover their expenses.

- More than a quarter of Gen Zers (26 percent) and millennials (31 percent) are not confident they will be able to retire comfortably.

- Around three-quarters of Gen Zers (72 percent) and millennials (77 percent) agree that the gap between the richest and poorest people in their country is widening.

Compare this to the older generations' top concerns. Both boomers and Gen Xers are concerned about retirement. The typical Gen Xer in 2007 had fewer financial assets—in the form of money held in savings accounts, 401(k)s, pensions and individual retirement accounts—than baby boomers held at the same age.

- From 2007 to 2010, Gen Xers lost nearly half their wealth, an average of about $33,000.

- Gen Xers are not on track for a secure retirement.

- Eighty-nine percent of Gen Xers have debt—averaging $103,800 per household.

- Gen Xers have the highest rate of economic mobility "stickiness"—meaning the relative rate of their economic status compared to their parents. About 40 percent of those raised by low-income parents remain low income themselves, and about 40 percent of those raised by high-income parents end up high income.

- It's been reported that 76 percent of older workers see age discrimination as a hurdle to finding a new job. Additionally, more than half of these older workers are prematurely pushed out of longtime jobs, and 90 percent of them never earn as much again.

When considering the social, economic and racial influences of these different generations, it should come as no surprise that they need different treatment in the workplace to function well and feel included.

The Age Gap Is Real

All sorts of gaps appear in the news. Wage gap. Attention gap. Gender gap. Reality gap.

The graph below is taken from an organization that took the Spectra Assessment, and you can probably spot this gap right away. This company has a significant generation gap in their talent pool. Nearly 29 percent of their employees are age 25–34 (combination Gen Z and millennials) and another 29 percent are 55–64 (combination Gen X and baby boomers). You could look at it another way: the parents and their children.

What is your age?

Age Group	Percentage
18 to 24 (1.45%)	
25 to 34 (28.99%)	
35 to 44 (17.39%)	
45 to 54 (14.49%)	
55 to 64 (28.99%)	
65 to 74 (2.9%)	
Prefer not to answer (5.8%)	

0%   5%   10%   15%   20%   25%   30%   35%

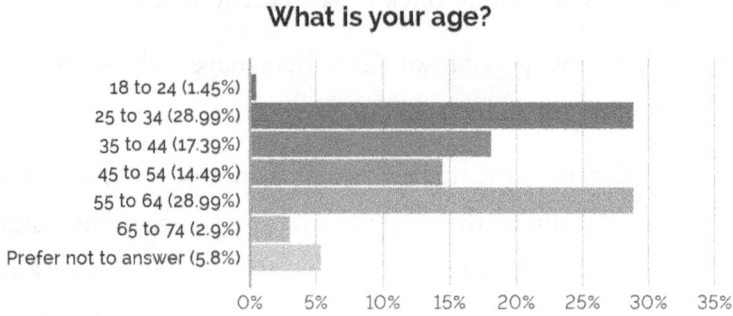

Not only are the work styles of the age groups different—their impressions of the DEI efforts of their organization's management, culture and 3 *P*s (policies, practices and procedures) were not only different—but statistically significant in their differences.

When Spectra Diversity provides data reports to our clients and partners, we have color coded the demographic lines that are statistically different. In the recreated graphic below, the yellow demographic is the norm—and the gray-highlighted demographic line is one which is statistically different. The data shown below is for a small organization—just sixty-nine responses—and yet the difference is stark.

"Management holds all employees equally accountable for their actions and behaviors."

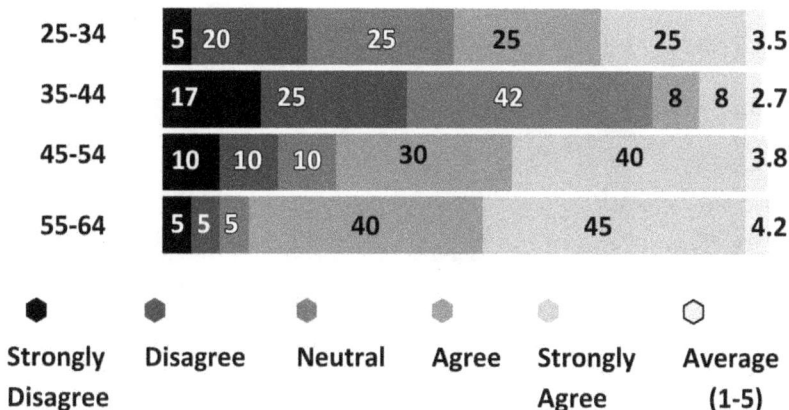

Age	Strongly Disagree	Disagree	Neutral	Agree	Strongly Agree	Average (1-5)
25-34	5	20	25	25	25	3.5
35-44	17	25	42	8	8	2.7
45-54	10	10	10	30	40	3.8
55-64	5	5	5	40	45	4.2

On the statement "Management holds all employees equally accountable for their actions and behaviors," notice that 85 percent of the oldest generation either agreed or strongly agreed with that statement, in contrast to only 16 percent of the thirty-five- to forty-four-year-olds. This organization's younger employees were also significantly lower in their average score (2.7) compared to those of the same age in the same industry (3.7). Consider that the youngest employees are more likely to be at the lower wage scale—and could be more diverse. What are you doing to retain those employees?

When presenting data to Spectra Partners or clients, I always point out that the data tells us the what, but it does not tell us the why. However, if you don't measure—you don't know what to look for, much less why it is there. Here is another example from the culture segment of the same assessment.

"Disrespectful and noninclusive behavior is not tolerated at this organization."

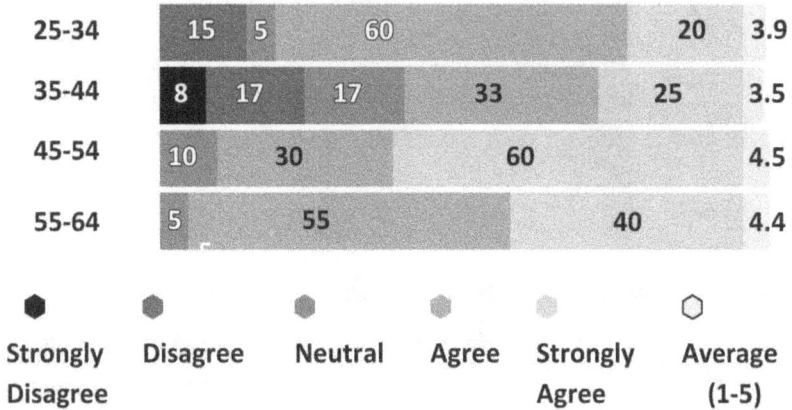

Age	Strongly Disagree	Disagree	Neutral	Agree	Strongly Agree	Average (1-5)
25-34	15	5	60		20	3.9
35-44	8	17	17	33	25	3.5
45-54	10	30		60		4.5
55-64	5	55		40		4.4

● ● ● ● ○ ○

Strongly Disagree   **Disagree**   **Neutral**   **Agree**   **Strongly Agree**   **Average (1-5)**

In this culture statement, the gap isn't quite as large (3.5 for the average of the younger generation compared to 4.4 of the older generation). However, 95 percent of the older generation agree with the statement "Disrespectful and noninclusive behavior is not tolerated at this organization," compared to 58 percent of the younger generation. In addition, the younger generation was lower than the industry comparison (3.5 compared to 4), and the older generation was higher than the industry average (4.4 compared to 4.2). Keep in mind that respect should be assumed for *all* generations—each of whom has something unique to offer.

This final comparison using this organization's data is in the policies, practices and procedures category.

"The HR policies, practices and procedures in this organization support diversity and inclusion."

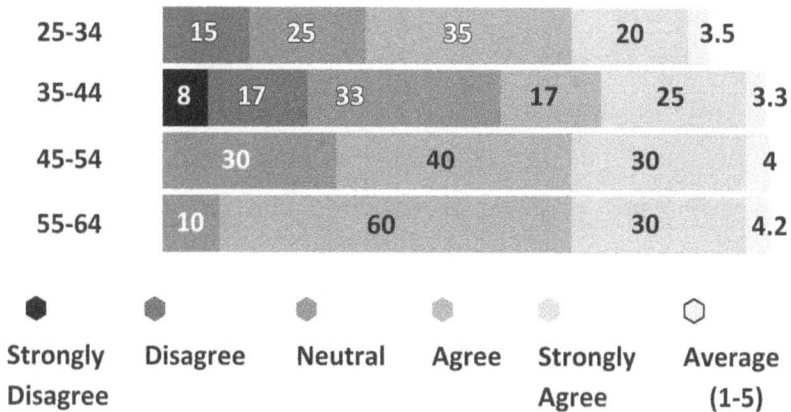

Age	Strongly Disagree	Disagree	Neutral	Agree	Strongly Agree	Average (1-5)
25-34	15	25	35	20		3.5
35-44	8	17	33	17	25	3.3
45-54		30	40	30		4
55-64		10	60	30		4.2

● Strongly Disagree   ● Disagree   ● Neutral   ● Agree   ● Strongly Agree   ○ Average (1-5)

In this statement, there is once again a significant split in how strongly the individuals felt about this statement. Ninety percent of the older generation either agreed or strongly agreed with the statement "The HR policies, practices and procedures in this organization support diversity and inclusion." This compares to 42 percent of the younger generation. Once again, there is also a gap in the younger generation compared to the same age group in its industry (3.3 compared to 3.9). Revising HR policies to consider generational differences is something that can change perceptions favorably and help retain employees on both ends of the age spectrum.

It takes a skilled psychometrician to be able to pull all this data together and have it be not only accurate but meaningful. It's also one of the reasons why it can be hard to create your own diversity and inclusion measurement device. It's challenging, specialized and time-consuming work.

. . . .

"In general, I feel age is one area that is overlooked when it comes to DEI initiatives not only at our organization but in industry as a whole. Although race, gender and sexual orientation are very important areas to address, ageism in our industry is especially rampant and has the potential to directly affect way more people as they move through their career."

—Anonymous

. . . .

LEARNING ACTIVITY

How Much Do You Know? (Answers in Appendix)

Since 2000, age discrimination cases have accounted for _____ of all EEOC cases.	36
Texas A&M reports a sharp drop in women's résumé ratings for candidates over ___, while male résumé ratings don't begin to drop until age fifty.	20%–25%
Nearly ____ workers aged 45 and older have been subjected to negative comments about their age from supervisors or coworkers.	6.3 million
There will be more people over ___ than under eighteen by 2035.	1 in 4
_____ cases of depression globally are estimated to be attributable to ageism. It intersects and exacerbates other forms of bias and disadvantage including those related to sex, race and disability.	65

Advice for Working with Millennials and Gen Z

This list below assumes that you are either a Gen X or a baby boomer who could use some tips for the younger generations.

- They respond to "lightweight signals" such as indirect inferences. Provide suggestions in soundbites—not a full movie.

- Facilitate, don't direct. Explain what to do—without dictating.

- Train them more. They grew up in a complex world so are very open to training and learning new skills.

- Reinforce the "why," because they tend to be better at perceiving value and weeding out the superfluous.

- Make it fun when you can, because you're competing with Instagram, Facebook, TikTok and other social media.

- Promote work-life integration. Promote healthy integration after hours.

- Make it fun. Again. Making the environment fun promotes productivity.

- Connect them to the mission. This is the "why" again. Show them how their project or task fits into the mission of the company.

- Be super clear about expectations. Give them the what and the why, and let them figure out the how-to-get-there.

- Always put things in context. Where does this fit in to their week and month? Why is this even important?

Advice for Working with Gen X And Baby Boomers

This list below assumes that you're one of the younger generations and can get frustrated working with elders.

- They respond to direct requests or instructions. Don't leave them hanging with "Whenever you can get to it."

- Don't assume they don't understand technology. Some don't. Some do. We're all wired differently.

- Respect their knowledge. Most didn't get to be where they are without picking up a significant amount of knowledge—or dare I say wisdom.

- Deadlines are OK. Most of us oldsters grew up with deadlines as a way of life. We're used to them.

- Don't expect them to socialize out of work. They may be caring for elderly parents or grandchildren, and time is at a premium.

- Do be patient. (If we repeat ourselves, just say thank you.)

- Don't expect them to check email outside of work. Some may do that—some don't.

- In general, an email is preferrable to a text. Getting pinged during the day is disruptive—so use sparingly. If something is really important, pick up the phone.

Leadership Strategies

What can you do to ensure your organization is inclusive of all generations? Here are some measures you, as a leader, can take.

- **Model appropriate behavior.** Reassure employees that it is really OK to take advantage of work-life policies you have in place. Telling employees to enjoy their evening, weekends or vacation is great. What is better is to "walk the talk" and refrain from sending emails and calling employees during times away from work.

- **Model diversity.** If you say you value diversity in the workforce, prove it by having diversity on your leadership team.

- **Avoid sending mixed messages.** Don't talk about policies or have them in an employee handbook when they aren't true. If you demonstrate that vacations are truly vacations, then be sure not to make employees feel like they are doing something wrong or that they should feel bad about taking a vacation. If you have "inclusion" in your organization's mission statement, make sure it is tied to accountability of the management team.

- **Assess team dynamics.** When you're conducting meetings, do you notice some people are contributing less? Do you need to draw out the younger team members? Do you need to acknowledge the experience of older team members? Work to understand how each person is being present based on their interactions.

- **Create guidelines and expectations.** Train management and employees on organizational policies and expectations. While managers may communicate in some way or another with employees after work hours without needing an immediate response, employees who get after hours calls or emails are more likely to feel pressured to respond after work as well.

- **Look for bias in your policies, practices and procedures.** When looking at your older employees, consider that a bad performance review can stick around as residue and rule an employee out for a promotion or key project assignment. Consider setting up a team of reviewers for promotions so that one individual doesn't have undue influence. Remember that most people identify with people who are like themselves—so include diversity on your team of reviewers.

Employers must encourage and support work-life policies if they want to remain competitive. Flexibility is key, particularly to millennials, but everyone benefits. Done right, employers and employees both benefit.

ACTION ITEMS

- ❑ Include measurement of age groups when conducting your diversity, equity and inclusion assessment.
- ❑ Foster inclusion by being aware of generational differences and accommodating them.
- ❑ Create intergenerational teams and foster inclusion by being a role model.

CHAPTER 9

Where Are All the Veterans?

As we express our gratitude, we must never forget that the highest appreciation is not to utter words but to live by them.

—JOHN F. KENNEDY

Veteran Data to Consider

When Spectra Diversity launched its assessment in 2017, we did not collect data on veteran status. We began doing so in 2020.

Demographic Group	Average score (out of 25)
Male	19.25
Veteran / Active Military	18.81
White / Caucasian	18.79
Hawaiian / Pacific Islander	18.71
Straight / Heterosexual	18.71
People without Disability	18.67
Hispanic / Latino	18.63
Not a Veteran	18.60
Asian	18.59
American Indian / Alaska Native	18.53
Female	18.16
People with Disability	17.74
Multiracial	17.49
Sexual Orientation - No Answer	17.45
LGBTQ	17.32
Disability - No Answer	17.15
Black / African American	16.87
Other / No Race	16.76
Non-binary / Third Gender	15.95
Veteran - Prefer Not to Answer	15.08

The chart above is from the Annual Spectra Assessment Report (ASAR) published in 2022. You can see that the demographic with the *most* favorable perceptions of management is the male with 19.25 out of 25 possible points. Right behind them are the veterans and active military personnel at 18.81, and nonveterans are further down the list at 18.6.

Veterans and active-duty military personnel are also placed high among the demographic categories in terms of their perceptions of organizational culture and their organization's policies, practices and procedures.

- In terms of professions, veterans who are employed are over-represented in the following fields:

  - Law enforcement

  - Construction

  - Local, state or federal government jobs

  - Manufacturing

  - Transportation

- The post-9/11 veterans are 17 percent women, compared to 4 percent women for WWII, Korea and Vietnam.

- Twenty-seven percent of veterans have a service-related disability.

- The VA has resources to help veterans with their careers.

- Veterans are 37 percent more likely to be underemployed than nonveterans.

Continuum of Service

PTSD %

37	80		30	12	20

Veterans in Millions

	6.262	1.689	3

WWII	Korean	Vietnam	Gulf	Iraq/Afghanistan
.389	1.165			

Noncombat Veterans' Stories

This has been a difficult chapter for me to write as a nonveteran and former war protester. Just as I do when trying to understand the thoughts, feelings and perspectives of a BIPOC individual or gay individual, I need to work to understand the perspectives of those who choose to put their lives on the line and potentially go to war.

I have some minor perspective because of the three veterans in my immediate family.

James—My Father

Born in 1927, my dad came of age during World War II and is alive and well as of this writing. He enlisted in the army and was part of the First Cavalry Division—military police. Yes—there was still a cavalry with horses. After basic training he was deployed as part of the Japanese invasion troops. He often jokes that Truman was the only Democrat he ever liked—because Harry dropped the bomb when my dad was training for the Japanese invasion. My dad ended up being part of the occupation troops. He was injured in a truck-rollover accident and was able to get disability because of an ear injury that led to deafness in one ear. He wears his WWII Veteran baseball cap often and smiles broadly when people thank him for his service.

Mark—My Brother

My brother enlisted in the marines after high school graduation and served in several posts around the world. While posted in Japan, he met his wife, whose father had fought in World War II on the Japanese side. My brother and his wife had three children by the time my brother had been in the marines for eighteen years. Mark's Japanese father-in-law and mother-in-law lived with my brother and his family for several years in the US and cared for their grandchildren. My brother's in-laws spoke no English—but managed to communicate with the limited Japanese my brother learned. The children were raised bilingual.

Peter—My Nephew

Like his father, Peter enlisted in the marines after high school gradua-tion and has been serving in several posts around the world, primarily embassy duty. Like his father, he met his wife when stationed overseas. They have one child together, and he is still serving proudly with the US Marines. He looks incredibly dashing in his uniform blues. His safety is always on the minds of his family as armed conflict continues around the world.

The veterans in my family all enlisted. None of the veterans in my family have been involved in combat (to date). To understand the differences and how being a combat veteran impacts one's life and whether the draft had an additional impact, I broadened my outreach for additional perspective.

Ron—Vietnam Vet

Ron is a colleague I met long after he served in Vietnam. Few people knew he was a Vietnam vet. He'd enlisted after dropping out of the junior college he'd been attending. Without the college deferment, he preferred enlistment to being drafted, and so he joined the navy. He had three deployments on an aircraft carrier, where he was trained in electronics. "In Vietnam, you went in and out of service alone. You were the replacement person or the 'new guy' and had to stick it out until you were no longer the newbie." When he finished his time in the navy, he was warned to wear civilian clothes when traveling home.

When out, he went back to school and met his wife (of forty-eight years now) on his first day of class. Still, he didn't acknowledge his time in the service. In 2005 there was a memorial dedication in Chicago, and he went to it. A group of protesters were there: Viet Veterans Against the War. For the first time he felt pride and saw the power of the experience.

By the time I met him, he was a TV film instructor at Indiana University. "The structure in higher education lends itself to someone like me, who went to Catholic school and served in the military," he told me. "There is open dialogue, and you don't have to censor yourself. You try to fit in and follow the rules, but you also have more confidence in yourself and your skills."

Recently he has turned his video skills and his experience as a veteran into documentary filmmaking.

- *My Vietnam, Your Iraq*—shown on PBS

- *Just Like Me: Vietnam War Stories from All Sides*—Shown on PBS and winner of a Regional Emmy Award

View from the Perimeter

As I was collecting these stories, I was reminded of my former father-in-law. He enlisted in the army and fought in World War II. He was at the Battle of the Bulge and was one of the first soldiers to enter the Eagle's Nest. To refresh your history knowledge, Battle of the Bulge, also called Battle of the Ardennes, (December 16, 1944–January 16, 1945), was the last major German offensive on the western front during World War II—an unsuccessful attempt to push the Allies back from German home territory. The "bulge" refers to the wedge that the Germans drove into the Allied lines. It was a back-and-forth battle in fog, cold and snow that resulted in 75,000 Allied and 120,000 German casualties. My father-in-law never spoke of it.

Another potential interview subject declined to speak with me. He was a Vietnam vet who saw significant combat and suffers from PTSD to this very day.

Once again, recall that data tells us the what—but not the why. Hopefully we can shed a little light on the topic.

PTSD Stories

Robin—Vietnam Vet

Robin is the friend of a friend, born in 1943. Robin was in college during the era when young men were being drafted into Vietnam unless they had a college, medical or other type of deferment. Robin was flunking out of college, and his dad gave him some advice that he took: "Join the navy, son. You'll get a dry bunk and three square meals a day."

Robin's family had several nurses and doctors in its ranks, so Robin was inclined to follow that path and became a hospital corpsman.

The navy acts as the medical corps for the US Marines, and so Robin's training involved operation room training, field medical training and Marine training (patrols, ambush, weapons fire, etc.) When he shipped off to Vietnam on April 21, 1967, he had two sea bags—one with marine gear and one with navy gear. He was assigned to the Third Medical Battalion, Third Marine Division.

His job as a hospital corpsman in Vietnam meant round-the-clock shifts. Soon after arriving an activity began that would have a huge impact on Robin. Later it was given a name—the Tet Offensive. "For forty days and forty nights we worked for sixteen hours per day, with the next eight hours to sleep and then we'd start all over again." He said at times there were mortars dropped on the hospital—likely an overshoot because the hospital was near the airport. When mortars would hit the hospital or land close by, the operating crew would duck and cover—with the patient still on the table.

When he was back on US soil, he was on a bus leaving the [San Francisco area] base, and he wondered why there was wire on all the windows. He soon found out when war protesters with sticks struck the bus. The new veterans were warned to wear their civilian clothes. Robin kept his Vietnam service secret for many years as he went back to school and got a nursing degree. He retired as the head of nursing for a hospital in Minnesota.

Robin paused to collect himself several times as he told his story. He didn't realize he had PTSD until he went into therapy during a divorce twelve years after leaving Vietnam. Until then he had put his emotions in a box and hid them away. Since then, he has begun to share his story—it helps him to process—and has bought a Vietnam Veteran cap that he wears. "PTSD doesn't have a cure," he told me.

"All you can do is treat it." He has worked to be in touch with his emotions—specifically empathy, sympathy and horror.

"I believe that combat vets make good employees because they have self-discipline, they can work when scared or threatened and they follow the direction of people who are in authority."

Max—Three Tours in Iraq

Max is a good friend of my son. Max was one of the young men inspired at an early age by the events of 9/11. He watched the plane hit the second of the World Trade Center towers while in his high school classroom. Max enlisted in the army at the age of eighteen and served for seven years, achieving the rank of sergeant and completing three tours in Iraq. After release from the army, he spent an additional two-and-a-half years in Afghanistan as a contractor in intelligence and counterintelligence. After his time in Afghanistan, he was an intelligence instructor.

He enlisted originally with a group of thirty, all of whom were married at the time. Today, just two or three of the couples are still married. His own marriage ended in divorce, and with undiagnosed PTSD, he was drinking half a bottle of vodka per night. He sought help—which wasn't helpful until he found a psychologist who was also a veteran.

"It's hard for nonveterans to understand the stress of keeping a team of thirty people alive and being responsible for $10 million in highly specialized equipment. Nonveterans don't understand the incredible (drug-free) high of being in a firefight and coming out alive."

After release from the service, some veterans keep chasing that high with either drugs and alcohol or risky behavior. One of Max's friends went to Africa to protect animals from poachers—another dangerous job. "You get programmed to dehumanize the enemy so you can kill them. You don't get unprogrammed when you're out. You must do it on your own," said Max.

Unlike World War II and Vietnam, during Operation Iraqi Freedom (OIF) and Operation Enduring Freedom (OEF), "the volunteers were at war, and America was at the mall." The difference between this generation and earlier ones is that there is earlier help for PTSD diagnosis and treatment.

Max is in a good place right now. Unable to get a job that used his many skills, he went back to school and got a computer science degree. He is putting his leadership and technical skills to work for a national physical fitness organization. He loves his job and brings insights and perspectives to the table that his nonveteran coworkers likely couldn't.

"War changes you. You learn to own your mistakes and move on. I don't have a problem with rules—I lived under them for years. I don't get stressed out if I'm asked to come into the office three days per week—I say, 'Fine.' I was taught to think outside the box to problem-solve. I can manage different types of people—after all, I dealt with Afghan war lords. And I oversaw the lives of 30 other people under my command. I can handle responsibility."

Hank—Afghanistan, Helman Province

Hank is another of my son's good friends. Hank is six foot four and was on a full ride scholarship for Division I football. And like Ron, he felt himself floundering. Hank's dad was a US Marine—and so Hank selected the marines not too long after 9/11. Unlike in Vietnam, the deployments in Iraq and Afghanistan were organized as military units. Hank was one of the first US Marines in Afghanistan.

He was a machine gunner, which means he probably couldn't count how many individuals he shot and killed—and I didn't ask. As part of the "War Dogs" (Second Battalion, Seventh Marines Echo Company), he told me, "Once you're in the fight, you're fighting for your buddies. You have their back, and you know they have yours."

His unit had twenty-five KIAs (*KIA* means "killed in action") and more than two hundred wounded. His unit was also number one in terms of suicide, with seventy-three lost since 2011.

When Hank was released, he was in danger of following that same path—called a cluster effect. A suicide cluster is a group of suicides, suicide attempts or self-harm events that occur closer together in time and space than would normally be expected in each community.

What saved him was football. He was given another scholarship, this time to a Division II school. While there, he was the twentieth recipient of the prestigious Disney Sports Spirit Award. It was reported that "after a nine-month combat stint in Afghanistan in April 2008, Hank Goff struggled with post-combat trauma and post-traumatic stress disorder, which led to depression and excessive drinking. It was a dark period during which Goff said he felt like a monster. Goff credits football with helping him find his way back to the light. Today, at the advanced football age of 28, Goff has become a stellar Division II football player (this year, he was a preseason second-team All-American) who has begun to counsel fellow veterans coping with similar post-war challenges."

Hank still has some aftereffects from his time in the service. He has 80 percent disability because of nerve damage in his arm from an injury plus PTSD. He is currently married with two children (ages two and four) and is working in a sports management company and tech start-up company called Player's Health. Although he didn't know it when he was hired, his boss is also a veteran. He has a few theories on why veterans are typically happy with their employers. "You're used to being a part of a team," he told me. "You learn how to take direction. You learn to admit your mistakes when you make them and move on."

LEARNING ACTIVITY

How Much Do You Know? (Answers in Appendix)

The unemployment rate for veterans who served on active duty in the US Armed Forces at any time since September 2001—a group referred to as Gulf War–era II veterans—rose to ____ percent in 2020.

18

The demographic profile of veterans is expected to change in the next quarter century. About nine in ten veterans (89 percent) are men, while about one in ten (11 percent) are women. By 2046, the share of female veterans is expected to increase to about ____ percent.

7.3

Veterans accounted for 5,989 suicides in 2001, which represented ____ percent of suicides among US adults.

30

High veteran unemployment is caused by poor health, selection, employer discrimination, skills mismatch or job search. Of these five possible causes, only ____ speaks to the short-term spike in unemployment found in recent data on veterans newly separated from the military.

20.2

____ percent of active duty and reserve military personnel deployed in Iraq and Afghanistan have a mental health condition requiring treatment.

job search

Thank You for Your Service

During my discussions with these veterans, I was very clear that I am antiwar, prosoldier. The veterans I spoke to understand the difference. I asked each of them what they thought about being told "Thank you for your service." My dad once said, "You're welcome," to the food server who was waiting on us and then turned to whisper to me, "I didn't do s**t." Max said that he just says thank you and figures that most of the time people simply don't know what to say.

"Thank you for your service" may or may not mean anything. I liked Ron's advice. "After someone says, 'Thank you for your service,' they should ask a follow-up question. It can be anything. What branch were you in? Where did you serve? Were you in combat?" The follow-up question is the indication that you care.

Leadership Strategies

The Society of Human Resource Management (SHRM) has an excellent set of resources for recruiting and working with veterans. Here are a few tips:

- The Employer Support of the Guard and Reserve (ESGR) is an organization that acts as employers' advocates within the US Department of Defense (DOD). Reach out to a local representative to recruit National Guard and Reserve members.

- Do you have a military base nearby? They have community centers that would be a good outreach point for hiring.

- The Military Spouse Employment Partnership is a DOD-led initiative that connects military spouses with employers who have committed to recruit, hire, promote and retain military spouses. Check them out.

- If you're interviewing a veteran, be very clear about the job role, the responsibilities attached and the expectations you have for the role. Clarity is important here.

- After hiring, you may be eligible for the Work Opportunity Tax Credit (WOTC)—a federal tax credit available to employers for hiring individuals from certain target groups who have consistently faced significant barriers to employment.

- Brand your organization as veteran friendly in your recruitment and marketing materials.

- Veterans may have PTSD and may or may not disclose this fact. If they disclose their condition, inquire as to any accommodations they may need.

ACTION ITEMS

❑ Track your veteran numbers. Do you know how many you have? If not, measure.

❑ Recruit with inclusion in mind. There are millions of veterans ready for the workforce, and they should be excellent employees. One could be your next genius hire.

❑ Hire with leadership in mind as well as potential accommodation. Many vets won't need accommodations— although some will.

Final DEI Steps

A lot of different flowers make a bouquet.

—ISLAMIC PROVERB

Our Journeys Continue

Throughout this book we've been looking at ways to provide *power* to create an inclusive culture in organizations. Keep in mind that power isn't like apple pie. If you have a piece of it, it doesn't mean that I have less. Everyone has their own power, and collectively, a 25 percent change in the mindset of your employees can create the power to move your organization forward on the DEI journey.

We're all on our own diversity, equity and inclusion journey. We all have the power to move forward as individuals and as a group.

The following are additional ways you can harness power to create an inclusive culture in your organization.

The Power of Anticipation

Diversity is not how we differ. Diversity is about embracing one another's uniqueness.

—OLA JOSEPH

Diversity is not only about bringing different perspectives to the table. When you add demographic diversity to a group, it makes people believe that differences of perspective might exist among them, and that belief makes people change their behavior.

Members of a homogeneous group rest somewhat assured that they will agree with one another, that they will understand one another's perspectives and beliefs, that they will be able to easily come to a consensus. But when members of a group notice that they are socially different from one another, they change their expectations. They anticipate differences of opinion and perspective. They assume they will need to work harder to come to a consensus. This logic helps to explain both the upside and the downside of diversity; people work harder in diverse environments both cognitively and socially. They might not like it, but the hard work can lead to better outcomes.

In a 2006 study of jury decision-making, social psychologist Samuel Sommers of Tufts University found that racially diverse groups exchanged a wider range of information during deliberation about a sexual assault case than all-white groups did.

Consider the following scenario: You are writing up a section of a paper for presentation at an upcoming conference. You are anticipating some disagreement and potential difficulty communicating because your collaborator is American and you are Chinese. Because of one social distinction, you may focus on other differences between yourself and that person, such as their culture, upbringing and experiences—differences that you would not expect from another Chinese collaborator. How do you prepare for the meeting? Likely, you will work harder on explaining your rationale and anticipating alternatives than you would have otherwise.

Learning to work with coworkers who are different from yourself is not necessarily easy. Just like exercise, it takes time and commitment to achieve your goals. The same goes for diversity. We need diversity—in teams, organizations and society as a whole—if we are to change, grow and innovate. Remember the saying "No pain, no gain." We must learn the skills to improve our effectiveness in working with individuals who come from different cultural backgrounds.

How to Incorporate This Power

When you're creating teams or your managers are creating teams— look for the maximum number of differences in your groups. Try to account for the main variables such as race/ethnicity, age, gender identity, sexual orientation, age and veteran status. If you don't have enough diversity on a certain level, pull someone up for a seat at the table. Universities do this when they add student representatives to their governing boards.

The Power of Storytelling

It is a great shock at the age of five or six to find out that in a world of Gary Coopers, you are the Indian.

—JAMES BALDWIN

Everyone has a diversity story. Think of the first time you knew you were different in some way. For me it is when I was laughed at for wearing glasses in grade school. For others it may be when they realized that their clothes were hand-me-downs rather than bought new. For still others it could be when they were called a racist slur— when they were too young to even know the meaning of it. Most of our first diversity stories happen when we are young. Others can hit us at a later age.

When you tell your diversity story as a leader, it can bring you closer to those around you and create a bridge that did not exist before. You are showing your vulnerability and building trust. You are modeling the inclusive behavior you want to see in others.

Storytelling is a critical strategic skill in the workplace. Keith Quesenberry, a researcher at Johns Hopkins University, says, "People are attracted to stories because we're social creatures, and we relate to other people."

It's no surprise. We humans have been communicating through stories for upward of twenty thousand years, back when our flat screens were cave walls.

Storytelling evokes a strong neurological response. Neuroeconomist Paul Zak's research indicates that our brains produce the stress hormone cortisol during the tense moments in a story and release oxytocin, the feel-good chemical that promotes connection and empathy. Other neurological research tells us that a happy ending to a story triggers the limbic system, our brain's reward center, to release dopamine that makes us feel more hopeful and optimistic.

Tell your story, and build connections with your leadership team and your employees.

How to Incorporate This Power

Below is a short exercise that you can use to foster storytelling in team meetings. The purpose of this activity is to

- demonstrate the importance of listening and respect,

- elicit empathy,

- demonstrate the power of storytelling and

- help each other gain new perspectives.

LEARNING ACTIVITY

This can be done in a group of six or so people. If you have ten or more people, divide them in half.

Using a blank piece of paper, allow approximately two minutes for people to write down their stories:

1. Describe the first time in your life growing up when you realized you were different in some way.

2. Describe a time during your career when you realized that you were different in some way.

Give the group the following ground rules:

*   Absolutely no talking (including *uh-huh*, *wow* or *oh dear*) when others are telling their stories.

*   What is shared here today does not leave this room.

*   Show respect by creating this as a safe place to share.

*   Each person will have three minutes to share their two stories.

*   Three minutes of time must be filled.

Ask for a volunteer to go first. If someone doesn't go first, then you do so and serve as a role model. Be brave. As the leader, you will be the timer. Continue until everyone has shared their two stories.

You can debrief this activity by asking the following questions:

*   How hard was it to fill three minutes?

*   What sorts of things did you learn about the others that you didn't know?

*   Was it easier for each successive person to share?

*   Any aha moments?

The Power of Neuroscience

*An individual has not started living until he can
rise above the narrow confines of his individualistic
concerns to the broader concerns of all humanity.*

—MARTIN LUTHER KING JR.

Our brains are plastic. The neuroplasticity of our brains means that we can rewire them to make old "biased" paths less strong compared to our new "updated" wiring. Neuroscience shows that our brains can yield positive results through the simple act of appreciation.

There was a study done in London in 2006 that showed London taxi drivers have a larger hippocampus (temporal lobe) than London bus drivers. Why? Because the hippocampus helps form and access complex memories, including spatial memories necessary to navigate efficiently. The taxi drivers must learn the streets (complicated), whereas the bus drivers had to learn a limited set of routes.

Bilinguals have been shown to have plasticity, perhaps due to the constant switching in their brains as they translate silently back and forth. The left inferior parietal cortex is larger in bilingual brains than in monolingual brains.

Musicians also show plasticity. A study compared professional musicians who practice at least one hour per day to amateur musicians and nonmusicians. It seems the volume of the cortex was highest in professional musicians, intermediate in amateur musicians and lowest in nonmusicians.

Neuroplasticity isn't just for experts in a field. For example, since turning fifty, I've learned how to create WordPress websites, how SEO affects a blog post, how to conduct statistically validated surveys and an awful lot about PowerPoint. And I'm now an amateur birder.

Turn yourself into a lifelong learner. It's fun!

How to Incorporate This Power

Neuroscience shows that our brains can yield positive results through the simple act of appreciation by adopting these three practices:

1. Build strong habits of appreciation.

    □ Get good at compliments.

    □ Cultivate and model the emotions you want others to have.

    □ Change the Golden Rule to the Platinum Rule: The Golden Rule is "Do unto others as you would have them do unto you." The Platinum Rule is "Do unto others as they wish to have done to them."

2. Make unfamiliar differences more familiar.

    □ Meet the people, not the stereotype or assumption in your head.

    □ Use storytelling and find connections.

3. Make expectations positive and explicit.

    □ Hold and communicate high expectations.

    □ Expand your circle of go-to people.

The Power of Inclusion

We all do better when we all do better.

—PAUL WELLSTONE

When you're working on inclusion in your organization, you must take everyone with you. If you don't bring everyone with you, you're running the risk of more divisiveness. Here I'm thinking of older people and white men. The last thing you need is men being labeled as male, pale and stale. Just as everyone has their own diversity story, we all have our own inclusion story.

Personally, I remember the feeling of not being included when I was working on a contract job and the area around my cube grew quiet. Where did everyone go, I wondered? I went to the company cafeteria, and there was my new group. Eating lunch together. Without me.

Diversity alone doesn't get the job done. If you're hiring for racial diversity, for example, you'll just lose the new hires if you don't have a culture of inclusion.

How To Incorporate the Power of Inclusion

Look back to the "How diverse is your universe?" activity in chapter 2. The ten people you trust can be the start of your new potential universe. These are the people with whom you can make additional connections to foster a sense of belonging and inclusion with more people. How can you make the connection?

- Ask someone to lunch (and consider any possible COVID-19 restrictions, of course).

- Ask someone who is not like you for a business or personal referral—a CPA, piano tuner or lawn-service company.

- Find out something about the people who are not like you, and ask to join them in a social activity (book club, baseball game or yoga lessons).

- Attend events that draw people who are different from you.

- Hire for diversity and then foster inclusion in your organization by being a role model.

The Power of Leadership

Good leadership requires you to surround yourself with people of diverse perspectives who can disagree with you without fear of retaliation.

—DORIS KEARNS GOODWIN

Statements in support of inclusion from yourself, as a CEO or other C-suite executive, are essential to developing the diversity, equity and inclusion that can drive your organization to new levels. However, comments aren't enough. Your involvement can't be for appearances only. A letter to employees or posting on the company website is not enough. There must be an ongoing informed conversation among those at the top who are using DEI data in their decision-making.

This isn't a one-and-done activity. And you don't get DEI data without measurement.

Remember that everyone is diverse in some way. If you're a manager, team leader or C-suite executive, the following are signs that you're doing it right. An inclusive leader is one who

- models the proper behavior for being inclusive,

- understands why and how inclusion is important to the organization,

- accepts and supports team/organizational decisions with grace and dignity,

- utilizes the unique skills, abilities and experience of all employees to achieve business results,

- builds teams that reflect a variety of opinions, experiences and thoughts and

- takes personal responsibility for their own outcomes.

How to Incorporate This Power

As an inclusive leader, please be aware of these insights about leadership and bias:

- The bias of very powerful individuals is magnified. This means *you*.

- Bias is often part of a process or system, usually unintentionally. An assessment can be a good way to root out this bad behavior.

- Biases that are in the historical culture of your organization can continue to have an impact. I've seen this recently in a bank that had a dress code from the 1980s.

So what can you do to foster inclusion? Reread chapter 3 in this book; there's one hint. Here are some additional tips:

- Consider tying leadership bonus to DEI metrics.

- Include DEI as a key performance indicator in your annual report.

- If you don't have a BIPOC individual on your board of directors, make room for at least two.

- Draw on the leadership strengths that we covered in chapter 3:

  - Emotional intelligence

  - Resilience

  - Trust

The Power of Measurement

Diversity is a fact, but inclusion is a choice we make every day. As leaders, we have to put out the message that we embrace and not just tolerate diversity.

—NELLIE BORRERO

I like to think that if you get data in front of people, they can get excited about it. If you start showing your people data, the enthusiasm starts to build. (How are we doing now? What is the third quarter looking like?) Nobody is going to come to you and say, "Please don't give me any data that will make our organization more innovative." If you can get employees excited about contributing to the data—even better. The data tells the story, and the story is the memorable part.

Here's a bit of new information: Understand the difference between a measure and a metric.

- A measure is one quantitative number that counts something (e.g., We made $100,000 profit last quarter).

- A metric gives you more information because it compares the measure to some other baseline (e.g., We made $100,000 profit last quarter, $50,000 more than the same quarter last year).

As you move forward on your DEI journey, you're going to be working on performance metrics (how are we doing right now in terms of DEI) and outcome metrics (how did we do compared to last year in terms of inclusion).

You'll also be looking at the stories behind the measurement.

- Why are the older employees disenchanted with the organization's culture?

- Why are the younger employees less positive about management?

- Why can't our organization keep Black women in our workforce?

- Why are veterans and those with disabilities so reluctant to self-disclose their status?

Data is a measurement of what. You are charged with discovering the why—and then doing something about it. Remember to collect both qualitative and quantitative data.

How to Incorporate This Power

With all that you've just learned about the different types of noninclusion that might be happening within your organization—you may have realized that there is a lot of work to do. But you can do it. The only way to really know what's going on—and to begin your diversity, equity and inclusion journey—is with *measurement*.

A statistically validated measurement tool will allow you to

- have a clear understanding of the diversity and inclusion strengths and opportunities that currently exist,

- have a solid foundation and measurement of employees' beliefs and attitudes regarding the organization's culture; management; and policies, practices and procedures,

- provide employees with an understanding of their individual beliefs and interpersonal skills related to diversity and inclusion,

- offer opportunity for leaders to design an action plan to move diversity, equity and inclusion efforts forward and

- measure improvement with subsequent assessments in future years.

What gets measured gets done.

Our ability to reach unity in diversity will be the
beauty and the test of our civilization.

—MAHATMA GANDHI

Here's your chance to write in this book and keep it as a reminder. Based on what you know now, what are three things you will start doing (that you're not currently doing), stop doing (because it is harmful or ineffective) or continue doing (because it's a good and effective thing to do)?

Remember that inclusion is the force that encourages diversity to thrive.

Start

1. _____
2. _____
3. _____

Stop

1. _____
2. _____
3. _____

Continue

1. _____
2. _____
3. _____

How Much Do You Know: Chapter One

1. The multiracial population was measured at 9 million people in 2010 and is now 33.8 million people in 2020, a 276 percent increase.

2. The "Some Other Race" alone or in combination group (49.9 million) increased 129 percent, surpassing the Black or African American population (46.9 million) as the second-largest race alone or in combination group (compared to white/Caucasian).

3. In a study of 506 US-based businesses, each 1 percent increase in the rate of gender diversity resulted in an approximately 3 percent increase in sales revenues, up to the rate represented in the relevant population.

4. 61 million adults in the United States live with a disability. Twenty-six percent of adults in the United States have some type of disability.

5. In 2018, women earned 44.7 percent of master's degrees and 41.2 percent of doctoral degrees.

YOUR RANKING (1–10)	AVERAGE RANKING (OTHER SMBS)	SURVEY STATEMENT
	8	I understand what diversity, equity and inclusion means at our organization.
	7.4	Management has created a culture of diversity, equity and inclusion.
	7.6	Management shows that diversity is important through their actions.
	7.6	Effort is made to solicit ideas from all employees.

How Much Do You Know: Chapter Two

1. Adding "salary negotiable" to job postings successfully reduced the gender gap in applications by 45 percent.

2. Research shows that the best way to remedy the effect of our implicit bias is to immerse ourselves in opportunities to make positive connections with a diverse group of people and to experience situations that put us outside our comfort zone.

3. In 2015, Hispanic people had $1.5 trillion in buying power, a staggering 50 percent increase from 2010.

4.   Companies ranking in the top quartile of executive-board diversity had ROEs 53 percent higher, on average, than companies in the bottom quartile.

5.   A University of Chicago empirical study indicated that people with more diverse sources of information generate consistently better ideas.

How Much Do You Know? Chapter Three

1.   Ninety-three percent of leaders agreed that the D&I agenda is a top priority, but only 34 percent believed that it's a strength in their workplace. In another survey, 80 percent of HR professionals viewed companies as "going through the motions."

2.   In 2018, fifty-one companies in the S&P 500 included a diversity metric in their compensation program. By February 2021, that number had nearly doubled to ninety-nine companies.

3.   Companies that disclosed EEO-1 reports outperformed their Russell 1000 peers in the stock market by 2.4 percent in 2021.

4.   Seventy-three percent of Americans want companies to publicize the ethnic and racial makeup of their organization.

5.   Forty-one percent of CEOs believe the lack of trust in their organization lies in their diversity, equity and inclusion practices.

How Much Do You Know? Chapter Four

1. Among S&P 500 companies, researchers found that boards were "gaming diversity" to please potential critics by appointing exactly two women to their boards. Forty-five percent more boards include exactly two women. (Deemed as "twokenism.")

2. Twelve percent of millennials (35 percent of the US workforce) identify as trans or nonbinary (double those from Gen X). Cisgender employees make 32 percent more money a year than transgender employees.

3. Women are more likely to be hired with blind applications, which increased the likelihood that a woman would be hired by between 25 and 46 percent.

4. Without diverse leadership, women are 20 percent less likely than straight white men to win endorsement for their ideas.

5. White men who experienced social disadvantages in the workplace based on socioeconomic status, disability, age, sexual orientation or religion are more likely than their white male counterparts who had not experienced such disadvantages to recognize white privilege.

How Much Do You Know? Chapter Five

1. Forty-eight percent of Generation Z are racial or ethnic minorities.

2. People who identify as white non-Hispanic in the United States declined in numbers for the first time on record, falling below 58 percent of the country's population in 2020.

3. By 2065, the US population will not have any single ethnic or racial majorities.

4. Of companies on the S&P 500, 29.6 percent do not have at least one Black board member. Today, there are five Black CEOs in the Fortune 500.

5. Without diverse leadership, People of Color are 24 percent less likely than straight white men to win endorsement for their ideas.

How Much Do You Know? Chapter Six

1. One in eight lesbian, gay and bi people (12 percent) wouldn't feel confident reporting any homophobic or biphobic bullying to their employer. One in five trans people (21 percent) wouldn't report transphobic bullying in the workplace.

2. Without diverse leadership, those who identify as LGBTQ are 21 percent less likely than straight white men to win endorsement for their ideas.

3. Among LGBTQIA+, 42 percent in these communities reported having been discriminated against because of their sexual orientation, and 16 percent reported they had lost their job because of it.

POWERING INCLUSIVE CULTURES

4. Roughly 52 percent of gay men aged 25 or older in the US hold a bachelor's degree, according to new research published in the American Sociological Review, far higher than the national average of 36 percent.

5. More than half of LGBTQ adults (54.6 percent) identify as bisexual. About a quarter (24.5 percent) say they are gay, with 11.7 percent identifying as lesbian and 11.3 percent as transgender.

Aging Quiz: Chapter Eight

1. It is possible to improve some of the memory loss often experienced by the elderly.

   True—Memory loss can be caused by conditions which are treatable such as poor nutrition, depression, loneliness, blood disorders, overmedication or the interaction of medications. By correcting the underlying condition, memory may be improved.

2. Most older adults become senile or demented.

   False—Only 30 percent of those over age eighty-five have any dementia. Aging by itself produces no decline in mental functioning except that short-term memory has a more limited capacity. Registering information may be slower, and learning may take longer. Concentration is better, and problem-solving skills improve.

3. Falling is one of the major causes of injury in older adults.

   True—Falls are the leading cause of accidental injury and the sixth leading cause of death in seniors. Falls occur most often in the bathroom and may be related to physical changes of aging, including mobility problems and visual changes, as well as the overuse or interaction of medications. Poor lighting, scatter rugs and unsafe bathroom equipment also contribute to falls.

4. Twenty-five percent of all persons over age sixty-five live in institutions.

   False—Most older persons live in their own homes. Although there are regional differences in the percentage of elderly persons living in institutions, the national average is only 10 percent.

5. Depression is a serious problem for older adults.

   True—Up to 15 percent of elderly women may suffer from depression. Depression, loss of self-esteem, loneliness and anxiety can become more common as older people face retirement. Multiple losses such as death of a spouse, friends or other crises often occur around the same time. Fortunately, depression is treatable.

6. Personality changes with age.

   False—Personality doesn't change with age, and all older people can't be described as rigid or difficult. You are what you are for as long as you live. However, you can always change your habits for the sake of your health.

7. Stress in a caregiver's life is rarely a factor for triggering abuse of an older adult.

    False—Family caregivers often experience physical, emotional and financial pressures when caring for an older relative. The stresses of caring for an older person who has health problems, when combined with unresolved personal issues and other responsibilities (such as work or child rearing), may lead to a potentially abusive situation. There are many community-support services that can help reduce caregiver burden and allow the older person to increase their independence.

8. Family members today do not provide as much care for their older relatives as they did in the past.

    False—Research shows that 80–90 percent of the care that older adults receive today is provided by family members.

Gen Z Quiz—Chapter Eight

All the statements in this quiz are true.

1. Gen Z is the last generation to have a white majority. A bare majority (52 percent) are non-Hispanic white—significantly smaller than the share of millennials who were non-Hispanic white in 2002 (61 percent). One in four Gen Zers are Hispanic, 14 percent are Black, 6 percent are Asian and 5 percent are some other race or two or more races.

2. Gen Z is generally progressive and progovernment. Fully seven-in-ten Gen Zers say the government should do more to solve problems. Roughly half of Gen Zers (48 percent)

and millennials (47 percent) say gay and lesbian couples being allowed to marry is a good thing for our society.

3. Gen Z is more likely to be children of immigrants compared to millennials. Twenty-two percent of Gen Zers have at least one immigrant parent, compared with 14 percent of millennials.

4. Gen Z is on track to become the most educated generation yet. Among eighteen- to twenty-one-year-olds no longer in high school in 2018, 57 percent were enrolled in a two-year or four-year college. This compares with 52 percent among millennials in 2003 and 43 percent among members of Gen X in 1987.

5. Gen Z is the first truly digital generation. They are digital natives who have little or no memory of the world as it existed before smartphones.

6. Gen Z is more likely to have college-educated parents compared to millennials. In 2019, 44 percent of Gen Zers ages 7 to 17 were living with a parent who had a bachelor's degree or more education, compared with 33 percent of millennials when they were the same age.

7. Gen Z are less likely to be working during their teen years compared to previous generations. Only 18 percent of Gen Z teens (ages 15 to 17) were employed in 2018, compared with 27 percent of millennial teens in 2002 and 41 percent of Gen Xers in 1986.

8. Gen Z agrees with millennials that climate change is due to human activity. These younger generations are more likely

than their older counterparts to say the earth is getting warmer due to human activity: 54 percent of Gen Z and 56 percent of millennials say this, compared with smaller shares of Gen Xers, boomers and Silents (48 percent, 45 percent and 38 percent, respectively).

How Much Do You Know? Chapter Seven

1. One in four adults in the US have some type of disability (26 percent). The percentage of people living with disabilities is highest in the South (US).

2. The 2021 jobless rate for those with a disability was about twice as high as the rate for those without a disability. In 2021, 29 percent of workers with a disability were employed part time, compared with 16 percent for those with no disability.

3. The Department of Labor found that employers who supported those with disabilities saw a 90 percent increase in employee retention. (Offering reasonable accommodations is often significantly less costly than firing workers.)

4. Companies that prioritized the inclusion of individuals with disabilities were four times more likely to outperform their competitors in shareholder returns, and have, on average 28 percent higher revenue. That's double the net income and 30 percent higher profit margins.

5. Fifty-nine percent of accommodations cost absolutely nothing to make, while the rest typically cost only $500 per employee with a disability.

How Much Do You Know? Chapter Eight

1. Since 2000, age discrimination cases have accounted for 20–25 percent of all EEOC cases.

2. Texas A&M reports a sharp drop in women's résumé ratings for candidates over thirty-six, while male résumé ratings don't begin to drop until age fifty.

3. Nearly one in four workers aged forty-five and older have been subjected to negative comments about their age from supervisors or coworkers.

4. There will be more people over sixty-five than under eighteen by 2035.

5. 6.3 million cases of depression globally are estimated to be attributable to ageism. It intersects and exacerbates other forms of bias and disadvantage including those related to sex, race and disability.

How Much Do You Know? Chapter 9

1. The unemployment rate for veterans who served on active duty in the US Armed Forces at any time since September 2001—a group referred to as Gulf War–era II veterans— rose to 7.3 percent in 2020.

2. The demographic profile of veterans is expected to change in the next quarter century. About nine in ten veterans (89 percent) are men, while about one in ten (11 percent) are

women. By 2046, the share of female veterans is expected to increase to about 18 percent.

3. Veterans accounted for 5,989 suicides in 2001, which represented 20.2 percent of suicides among US adults.

4. High veteran unemployment is caused by poor health, selection, employer discrimination, skills mismatch or job search. Of these five possible causes, only job search speaks to the short-term spike in unemployment found in recent data on veterans newly separated from the military.

5. Thirty percent of active duty and reserve military personnel deployed in Iraq and Afghanistan have a mental health condition requiring treatment.

AARP Staff, "4 Things Millennials Need to Know About Age Discrimination," AARP, January 25, 2021, https://www.aarp.org/work/age-discrimination/what-millennials-should-know/.

AARP Staff, "Age Discrimination Common in Workplace, Survey Says," AARP, August 2, 2018, https://www.aarp.org/work/age-discrimination/common-at-work/.

Accenture Staff, "Getting to Equal: The Disability Inclusion Advantage," Accenture, 2018, https://www.accenture.com/t20181029t185446z__w__/us-en/_acnmedia/pdf-89/accenture-disability-inclusion-research-report.pdf.

American Writers Museum Staff, "Themed Guided Exploration: Asian American and Pacific Islander Heritage Month," American Writers Museum, accessed July 28, 2022, https://americanwritersmuseum.org/program-calendar/themed-guided-exploration-asian-american-and-pacific-islander-heritage-month/.

Anderson-Finch, Shannon, and Nicole Patterson, "Inclusive Mobility: How Mobilizing a Diverse Workforce Can Drive Business Performance," Deloitte, 2018, https://www2.deloitte.com/content/dam/Deloitte/us/Documents/Tax/us-tax-inclusive-mobility-mobilize-diverse-workforce-drive-business-performance.pdf.

Annabi, Hala, Sarah Lebovitz, "Improving the Retention of Women in the IT Workforce: An Investigation of Gender Diversity Interventions in the USA," *Info Systems Journal* 28 (November 2018): 1049–1081.

Associated Press, "Back to Starbucks: Howard Schultz Returns as Interim Leader," Al Jazeera, March 16, 2022, https://www.aljazeera.com/economy/2022/3/16/back-to-starbucks-howard-schultz-returns-as-interim-leader.

Bagley, Betsy, "The Key D&I Success Factor: Getting your Leaders on Board," Pulsely White Papers, July 2020, https://assets-global. website-files.com/5ecd00fbbff1d943cb35a59e/5f16da1e8e64d17eedf a49f9_200720_pulsely_white-papers_the-key-di-success.pdf.

BBC UK Staff, "Scans See 'Gay Brain Differences," BBC One Minute News, June 16, 2008, http://news.bbc.co.uk/2/hi/health/7456588. stm.

Blanche, Aubrey, "Workplace Diversity, Equity, & Inclusion Report: Understanding the DEI Landscape," Cultureamp. https:///2022-workplace-dei-report.pdf.

Blumberg, Yoni, "Companies with More Female Executives Make More Money—Here's Why," CNBC, March 2, 2018, https://www.cnbc. com/2018/03/02/why-companies-with-female-managers-make-more-money.html.

Bonta, Emily, and Mona Patni, "Companies Disclosing the Highest Level of Workforce Diversity Data – EEO-1 Report – Saw Higher 2021 Returns," Just Capital, February 8, 2022, https://justcapital.com/ news/companies-sharing-eeo-1-data-saw-higher-returns/.

Bourke, Juliet, and Bernadette Dillon, "The Diversity & Inclusion Revolution," *Deloitte Review* 22 (January 2018): 82–95.

"Brain Drain: Why STEM Women Quit or Stagnate in Their Job," GoTARA, accessed March 16, 2023, https://www.gotara.com/ why-stem-women-quit-or-stagnate-in-their-job/.

Bureau of Labor Statistics Press Release, "Employment Situation of Veterans—2021," US Department of Labor, April 21, 2022, https:// www.bls.gov/news.release/pdf/vet.pdf.

Bureau of Labor Statistics Press Release, "Persons with a Disability: Labor Force Characteristics—2021," US Department of Labor, February 24, 2022, https://www.bls.gov/news.release/archives/ disabl_02242022.pdf.

Catalyst Editors, "Women in Management (Quick Take)," Catalyst, March 1, 2022, https://www.catalyst.org/research/women-in-management/.

Catt, Mary, "Disadvantage Impacts White Men's Perception of Privilege," *Cornell Chronicle*, February 1, 2022, https://news.cornell.edu/stories/2022/02/disadvantage-impacts-white-mens-perception-privilege.

Claudia, Deane, "Women and Leadership," Pew Research Center, January 14, 2015, https://www.pewresearch.org/social-trends/2015/01/14/women-and-leadership/.

Cohn, D'Vera, "Future Immigration Will Change the Face of America by 2065," Pew Research Center, October 5, 2015, https://www.pewresearch.org/fact-tank/2015/10/05/future-immigration-will-change-the-face-of-america-by-2065/.

College Evaluator, "Ivy League Members Comparison," College Evaluator, accessed July 28, 2022, https://www.collegeevaluator.com/ncaa-conferences/ivy-league/.

Cooperman, Alan, "Jewish Americans in 2020," Pew Research Center, May 11, 2021, https://www.pewresearch.org/religion/wp-content/uploads/sites/7/2021/05/PF_05.11.21_Jewish.Americans.pdf.

Cox, Gena, "5 Strategies to Infuse D&I into Your Organization," *Harvard Business Review*, May 19, 2021, https://hbr.org/2021/05/5-strategies-to-infuse-di-into-your-organization.

Currier, Erin, "How Generation X Could Change the American Dream," Pew Research, January 26, 2018, https://www.pewtrusts.org/en/trend/archive/winter-2018/how-generation-x-could-change-the-american-dream.

Custard, Martha Kendall, "34 Age Discrimination Facts That May Shock You and Your Workplace," Vervoe, June 7, 2022, https://vervoe.com/age-discrimination-facts/.

Davis, D. A. et al., "Accuracy of Physician Self-Assessment Compared with Observed Measures of Competence: A Systematic Review," *JAMA* 296, no. 9 (September 2006): 1094–1012.

Decision Lab Editors, "Why Can We Not Perceive Our Own Abilities?," The Decision Lab, accessed July 28, 2022, https://thedecisionlab.com/biases/dunning-kruger-effect.

Deloitte Global Staff, "Striving for Balance, Advocating for Change," Deloitte, 2022, https://www2.deloitte.com/content/dam/Deloitte/global/Documents/deloitte-2022-genz-millennial-survey.pdf.

Disability and Health Branch, "Disability Impacts All of Us," CDC, updated September 16, 2020, https://www.cdc.gov/ncbddd/disability-andhealth/infographic-disability-impacts-all.html#:~:text=61%20million%20adults%20in%20theis%20highest%20in%20the%20South.

Disability Integration Act Legislative Committee, "What Is the Disability Integration Act?," The Disability Integration Act, 2021, http://www.disabilityintegrationact.org/?fbclid=IwAR2iudZ6VJnSVrAOxfXN5E6btZUpY8nmqoear0_42jb3RYKM2UP0faEWtrQ.

Diversity & Inclusion Research Conference Organizers, "DIRC21 Content and Agenda," DIRC, Accessed July 28, 2022, https://dirc.info/.

Eastwood, Brian, "5 Digital Transformation and Talent Retention Ideas from MIT Sloan Management Review," MIT Management Sloan School, April 4, 2022, accessed March 16, 2023, https://mitsloan.mit.edu/ideas-made-to-matter/5-digital-transformation-and-talent-retention-ideas-mit-sloan-management-review.

Ehrman-Solberg, Kevin, "The Geography of Inequality," YouTube video, November 21, 2018, https://www.youtube.com/watch?v=Xi50RaTXrSE.

Ellis, Sarah Kate, "Accelerating Acceptance 2021: Executive Summary," GLAAD, January 2021, https://www.glaad.org/sites/default/files/AA2021_Final.pdf.

Ellsworth, Diana, Ana Mendy, and Gavin Sullivan, "How the LGBTQ+ Community Fares in the Workplace," June 23, 2020, https://www.mckinsey.com/featured-insights/diversity-and-inclusion/how-the-lgbtq-plus-community-fares-in-the-workplace.

Employment & Training Administration, "Work Opportunity Tax Credit," US Department of Labor, accessed July 30, 2022, https://www.dol.gov/agencies/eta/wotc.

Emthie23, "Moving from Autopilot to Mindfulness," CogBlog, November 24, 2020, https://web.colby.edu/cogblog/author/emthie,23/.

Everfi, "How to Avoid Age Discrimination in the Workplace," Blackbaud, accessed July 29, 2022, https://everfi.com/blog/workplace-training/how-to-avoid-age-discrimination-in-the-workplace/.

Ferman, Roy, "Why You Should Invest in Your Staff," Forbes, August 23, 2021, https://www.forbes.com/sites/forbesfinancecouncil/2021/08/23/why-you-should-invest-in-your-staff/?sh=315065863e58.

Ferreira, Trenise, "Hank Goff to Receive 2015 Disney Sports Spirit Award Thursday on ESPN," CSP Bears, December 9, 2015, https://cspbears.com/news/2015/12/1/FB_1201150145.aspx?path=football.

Finzi, Benjamin, "Summer 2022 Fortune/Deloitte CEO Survey," Deloitte, accessed July, 27, 2022, https://www2.deloitte.com/us/en/pages/chief-executive-officer/articles/ceo-survey.html.

Forman, Tami, "Women's Labor Force Participation Rate is 'Only' Down 1 Point Since Before the Pandemic. This Is Not Good News," LinkedIn, January 26, 2022, https://www.linkedin.com/pulse/womens-labor-force-participation-rate-only-down-1-point-tami-forman/.

Francis, David R., "Employers' Replies to Racial Names," *The Digest* 9 (September 2003), https://www.nber.org/digest/sep03/employers-replies-racial-names.

"Fortune/Deloitte CEO Survey: October 2020—Highlights," Deloitte, 2020, accessed March 16, 2023, https://www2.deloitte.com/content/dam/Deloitte/us/Documents/CMO/fortune-deloitte-CEO-survey-october-2020-highlights.pdf.

Gartner, "Home Page," Gartner: Human Resources, accessed July 28, 2022, https://www.gartner.com/en/human-resources/role/human-resources-leaders.

Gaser, Christian, and Gottfried Schlaug, "Brain Structures Differ between Musicians and Non-Musicians," *Journal of Neuroscience* 23, no. 27 (October 2003): 9240–9245.

Gender Decoder Creator, "Finding Subtle Bias in Job Ads," Gender Decoder, accessed on July 28, 2022, http://gender-decoder.katmatfield.com/.

Glass Lewis Editors, "Racial & Ethnic Diversity in the Boardroom," Glass Lewis, 2021, https://www.glasslewis.com/racial-ethnic-diversity-in-the-boardroom-glass-lewis-special-report/.

Glassdoor Team, "10 Ways to Remove Gender Bias from Job Descriptions," Glassdoor for Employees, April 2, 2021, https://www.glassdoor.com/employers/blog/10-ways-remove-gender-bias-job-listings/.

Goldin, Claudia, and Cecelia Rouse, "Orchestrating Impartiality: The Impact of 'Blind' Auditions on Female Musicians," *American Economic Review* 90, no. 4 (2000): 715–741.

Goleman, Daniel, *Emotional Intelligence: Why It Can Matter More Than IQ*, New York: Bantam Books, 2020.

Gura, David, "You Can Still Count the Number Of Black CEOs on One Hand," NPR, May 27, 2021, https://www.npr.

org/2021/05/27/1000814249/a-year-after-floyds-death-you-can-still-count-the-number-of-Black-ceos-on-one-ha#.

Hait, Andrew, "Number of Women-Owned Employer Firms Increased 0.6% from 2017 to 2018," United States Census Bureau, March 29, 2021, https://www.census.gov/library/stories/2021/03/women-business-ownership-in-america-on-rise.html.

Helfrich, Thomas, "How Diversity Can Help with Business Growth," *Forbes*, November 12, 2021, https://www.forbes.com/sites/forbestechcouncil/2021/11/12/how-diversity-can-help-with-business-growth/?sh=56e8d52652ad.

Hewlett, Sylvia Ann, Melinda Marshall, and Laura Sherbin, "How Diversity Can Drive Innovation," *Harvard Business Review*, December 2013, https://hbr.org/2013/12/how-diversity-can-drive-innovation.

History.com Editors, "Labor Movement," History.com, updated March 31, 2020, https://www.history.com/topics/19th-century/labor#section_10.

Horowitz, Juliana M, Ruth Igielnik, and Kim Parker, "Views on Leadership Traits and Competencies and How They Intersect with Gender," Pew Research Center, September 20, 2018, https://www.pewresearch.org/social-trends/2018/09/20/2-views-on-leadership-traits-and-competencies-and-how-they-intersect-with-gender/.

Horowitz, Juliana, "Most Americans say the Legacy of Slavery Still Affects Black People in the U.S. Today," Pew Research Center, June 17, 2019, https://www.pewresearch.org/fact-tank/2019/06/17/most-americans-say-the-legacy-of-slavery-still-affects-Black-people-in-the-u-s-today/.

Human Perspectives International Editors, "HPI's Resilience Tools," Resilience Human Perspective International, accessed July 28, 2022, https://www.hpiintl.com/solutions/assessments/hpi-resilience/.

Human Rights Campaign Foundation, "Glossary of Terms," HRC, accessed July 29, 2022, https://www.hrc.org/resources/glossary-of-terms.

Hunter-Gadsden, Leslie, "Chasing the Dream: The Troubling News about Black Women in the Workplace," PBS, November 8, 2018, accessed March 16, 2023, https://www.pbs.org/wnet/chasing-the-dream/stories/the-troubling-news-about-Black-women-in-the-workplace.

Hyder, Shama, "The Hidden Advantage of Women in Leadership," Inc., May 2, 2019, https://www.inc.com/shama-hyder/the-hidden-advantage-of-women-in-leadership.html.

Interlaw Diversity Forum, "LGBT+ Factsheet," Interlaw, 2020, https://5aa06e50-1b3c-4843-b70a-a841ab933579.usrfiles.com/ugd/5aa06e_b8150387ca1243418743b2b75f675414.pdf.

Jaffe, Greg, "A Rhodes Scholar Barista and the Fight to Unionize Starbucks," *Washington Post*, February 12, 2002, https://www.washingtonpost.com/nation/2022/02/12/rhodes-scholar-barista-fight-unionize-starbucks/.

Jan Publications, "Accommodation and Compliance: Interactive Process," Jan: Job Accommodation Network, accessed July 29, 2022, https://askjan.org/topics/interactive.cfm.

Jofee-Walt, Chana, "Nice White Parents," *New York Times* Podcast, July 17, 2020, https://nice-white-parents.simplecast.com/.

Johnson, Kevin, "Our Commitment to Inclusion, Diversity, and Equity at Starbucks," Starbucks Stories and News, October 14, 2020, https://stories.starbucks.com/stories/2020/our-commitment-to-inclusion-diversity-and-equity-at-starbucks/.

Johnson, Stephanie K., and Jessica F. Kirk, "Research: To Reduce Gender Bias, Anonymize Job Applications," *Harvard Business Review*, March 5, 2020, https://hbr.org/2020/03/research-to-reduce-gender-bias-anonymize-job-applications.

Jones, Chris, "Annual Spectra Assessment Report," Spectra Diversity, May, 2021, https://www.spectradiversity.com/wp-content/uploads/2021/05/Spectra-Diversity_Final.pdf.

Jones, Janelle, "5 Facts about the State of the Gender Pay Gap," US Department of Labor Blog, March 19, 2021, https://blog.dol.gov/2021/03/19/5-facts-about-the-state-of-the-gender-pay-gap.

Jones, Jeffrey M., "LGBT Identification in U.S. Ticks Up to 7.1%," Gallup, February 17, 2022, https://news.gallup.com/poll/389792/lgbt-identification-ticks-up.aspx.

Jones, Jeffrey M., "LGBT Identification Rises to 5.6% in Latest U.S. Estimate," Gallup, February 24, 2022, https://news.gallup.com/poll/329708/lgbt-identification-rises-latest-estimate.aspx.

Jones, Stacy, "White Men Account for 72% of Corporate Leadership at 16 of the Fortune 500 Companies," *Fortune*, June 9, 2017, https://fortune.com/2017/06/09/white-men-senior-executives-fortune-500-companies-diversity-data/.

Kirkland, Rik, and Iris Bohnet, "Focusing on What Works for Workplace Diversity," McKinsey & Company, April 7, 2017, https://www.mckinsey.com/featured-insights/gender-equality/focusing-on-what-works-for-workplace-diversity.

Kita, Joe, "Workplace Age Discrimination Still Flourishes in America," December 30, 2019, AARP, https://www.aarp.org/work/age-discrimination/still-thrives-in-america/.

Kline, Patrick, Evan Rose, and Christopher Walters, "Systemic Discrimination among Large US Employers," NBER Working Paper 29053 (February 2022): 1–111.

Kulik, Carol, Elissa L. Perry, and Anne C. Bourhis, "Ironic Evaluation Processes: Effects of Thought Suppression on Evaluations of Older Job Applicants," *Journal of Organizational Behavior* 21, no. 6 (September 2000): 689–711.

Kullgren, Ian, Brian Eckhouse, and Deena Shanker, "U.S. Labor Unions Are Having a Moment," Time.com, October 17, 2021, https://time.com/6107676/labor-unions/.

La Trobe University, "83% of Women Leave Their STEM Careers: We're Changing That," Nest, accessed July 27, 2022, https://www.latrobe.edu.au/nest/83-of-women-leave-stem/.

Larson, Erik, "Diversity + Inclusion = Better Decision Making at Work," Cloverpop, September 17, 2019, https://www.cloverpop.com/blog/infographic-diversity-inclusion-better-decision-making-at-work.

Lean In Editors, "Women in the Workplace Study," Lean In, 2021, https://leanin.org/women-in-the-workplace-report-2021/the-state-of-women-in-america.

LeanIn.org and McKinsey & Company, "Women in the Workplace 2021," Lean In, accessed March 16, 2023, https://leanin.org/women-in-the-workplace/2021/the-state-of-women-in-america

"LGBTQ Rights Timeline in American History," Teaching LGBTQ History: Instructional Resources for California Educators, Students, & Families, FAIR Education Act Implementation Coalition, accessed March 16, 2023, https://www.lgbtqhistory.org/lgbt-rights-timeline-in-american-history/.

Livingston, Gretchen, "Profile of U.S. Veterans is Changing Dramatically as Their Ranks Decline," November 11, 2016, https://www.pewresearch.org/fact-tank/2016/11/11/profile-of-u-s-veterans-is-changing-dramatically-as-their-ranks-decline/.

Livingston, Robert, "How to Promote Racial Equity in the Workplace," *Harvard Business Review*, September 2020, https://hbr.org/2020/09/how-to-promote-racial-equity-in-the-workplace.

Loughran, David S., "Why is Veteran Unemployment So High?," Rand Corporation, 2014, https://www.rand.org/pubs/research_reports/RR284.html.

Maguire, EA, Katherine Woollett, and Hugo Spiers, "London Taxi Drivers and Bus Drivers: A Structural MRI and Neuropsychological Analysis," *Hippocampus* 16, no. 12 (2006): 1091–101.

Mapping Prejudice Project, "About Mapping Prejudice," University of Minnesota, accessed July 28, 2022, https://mappingprejudice.umn.edu/about-us/project.

Markovits, Daniel, "Five Myths about Meritocracy," *Washington Post*, September 13, 2019, https://www.washingtonpost.com/outlook/five-myths/five-myths-about-meritocracy/2019/09/13/4d90d244-d4cd-11e9-9610-fb56c5522e1c_story.html.

Marsh, Jason, Rodolfo Mendoza-Denton, and Jeremy Adam Smith, *Are We Born Racist?: New Insights from Neuroscience and Positive Psychology*, Boston: Beacon Press, 2010.

Masterpiece Cakeshop v. Colorado Civil Rights Commission, Brief for National LGBTQ Task Force, October 30, 2017, https://www.the-taskforce.org/wp-content/uploads/2017/10/16-111-bsac-LGBTQ-Task-Force.pdf.

Mechelli, A. et al., "Structural Plasticity in the Bilingual Brain, *Nature* 431 (2004): 757.

Mental Health First Aid, "Veterans and Military," National Council for Mental Wellbeing, accessed July 30, 2022, https://www.mental-healthfirstaid.org/veterans-military/#.

Meshanko, Paul, *The Respect Effect: Using the Science of Neuroleadership to Inspire a More Loyal and Productive Workplace*, New York: McGraw-Hill Education, 2013.

Milkman, Katherine et al., "On the Board: Twokenism is the New Tokenism," *Washington Post*, November 3, 2018, https://www.wash-ingtonpost.com/business/2018/11/03/twokenism-is-new-tokenism/.

Miller, Claire Cain, "Is Blind Hiring the Best Hiring?," *New York Times*, February 25, 2016, https://www.nytimes.com/2016/02/28/magazine/is-blind-hiring-the-best-hiring.html.

Mittleman, Joel, "Intersecting the Academic Gender Gap: The Education of Lesbian, Gay, and Bisexual America," *American Sociological Review* 87, no. 2 (February 2022): 303–335.

Moon, Tanya, "Preliminary Information," Project Implicit, accessed July 29, 2022, https://implicit.harvard.edu/implicit/takeatest.html.

Morgan, Paula, "3 Reasons to Hire More Individuals with Disabilities in 2021," *Forbes*, December 16, 2020, https://www.forbes.com/sites/paulamorgan/2020/12/16/3-reasons-to-hire-more-individuals-with-disabilities-in-2021/?sh=28d775d93406.

Morrison, Tony, "Number of Adults Who Identify as LGBT Has Doubled in Past Decade, Study Finds," ABC News, February 17, 2022, https://abcnews.go.com/US/number-adults-identify-lgbt-doubled-past-decade-study/story?id=82961330.

National Center for Education Statistics, "Degrees Conferred by Race/Ethnicity and Sex," IES/NCES, accessed July 28, 2022, https://nces.ed.gov/fastfacts/display.asp?id=72.

National Center for Science and Engineering Statistics, "Field of Degree: Women," National Science Foundation, April 29, 2021, https://ncses.nsf.gov/pubs/nsf21321/report/field-of-degree-women.

National Human Genome Research Institute, "Genetics vs. Genomics Fact Sheet," Genome.gov, updated September 7, 2018, https://www.genome.gov/about-genomics/fact-sheets/Genetics-vs-Genomics#.

Ngun, Tuc, and Eric Vilain, "The Biological Basis of Human Sexual Orientation: Is There a Role for Epigenetics?," *Advanced Genetics* 86 (2014): 167–184.

Noland, Marcus and Tyler Moran, "Study: Firms with More Women in the C-Suite Are More Profitable," Peterson Institute for International Economics, February 8, 2016, accessed March 16, 2023, https://www.piie.com/commentary/op-eds/study-firms-more-women-c-suite-are-more-profitable.

Noland, Marcus, Tyler Moran, and Barbara Kotschwar, "Is Gender Diversity Profitable? Evidence from a Global Survey," Peterson Institute for International Economics, Working Paper 16, no. 3 (February 2016): 1–35.

Noonan, David, "The 25% Revolution—How Big Does a Minority Have to Be to Reshape Society?," *Scientific American*, accessed July, 27, 2022, https://www.scientificamerican.com/article/the-25-revolution-how-big-does-a-minority-have-to-be-to-reshape-society/.

Obi, Ifeoma, "Is Good Performance on the Job Determined by Degree Class," Industrial Psychology Consultants, March 2020, https://www.thehumancapitalhub.com/article/is-good-performance-on-the-job-determined-by-degree-class.

Orme, Ashely Marchand, "Big Companies Are Already Collecting Important Data on Workforce Diversity. More of Them Need to Make It Public," Yahoo! Finance, February 9, 2022, https://finance.yahoo.com/news/big-companies-already-collecting-important-103000936.html.

Osgood, Ron, "Home," Ron Osgood Personal Website, accessed July 30, 2022, http://www.ronosgood.com/.

Our Family Coalition, "LGBTQ Rights Timeline in American History," LGBTQ History, accessed July 29, 2022, https://www.lgbtqhistory.org/lgbt-rights-timeline-in-american-history/.

Parker, Kim, and Ruth Ingielnik, "On the Cusp of Adulthood and Facing an Uncertain Future: What We Know About Gen Z So Far," Pew Research Center, May 14, 2020, https://www.pewresearch.org/social-trends/2020/05/14/on-the-cusp-of-adulthood-and-facing-an-uncertain-future-what-we-know-about-gen-z-so-far-2/.

Parmelee, Michele, and Emma Codd, "Women @ Work 2022: A Global Outlook," Deloitte, 2022, https://www2.deloitte.com/content/dam/Deloitte/global/Documents/deloitte-women-at-work-2022-a-global-outlook.pdf.

Penn Medicine, "Brain Connectivity Study Reveals Striking Differences between Men and Women," *Penn Medicine News*, December 2, 2013, https://www.pennmedicine.org/news/news-releases/2013/december/brain-connectivity-study-revea.

People Management, "Diversity Drives Better Decisions," CIPD, July 28, 2022, https://www.peoplemanagement.co.uk/article/1742040/diversity-drives-better-decisions.

PeopleFluent Editors, "Measuring Diversity for Success," A PeopleFluent White Paper, 2015, https://www.slideshare.net/humancapitalmedia/measuring-diversity-for-success.

Peterson, Dana M., and Catherine L. Mann, "Closing the Racial Inequality Gaps: The Economic Cost of Black Inequality in the U.S.," Citi GPS, September, 20, 2018, https://www.citivelocity.com/citigps/closing-the-racial-inequality-gaps/.

Prabhakar, Kavitha et al., "Build Trust in Diversity, Equity, and Inclusion Commitments," Deloitte, January 13, 2022, https://www2.deloitte.com/us/en/insights/topics/talent/building-employee-trust-dei-programs.html.

Reiners, Bailey, "50 Diversity in the Workplace Statistics you Should Know," Built In, October 21, 2021, https://builtin.com/diversity-inclusion/diversity-in-the-workplace-statistics.

Ro, Christine, "How the Salary 'Ask Gap' Perpetuates Unequal Pay," BBC, June 18, 2021, https://www.bbc.com/worklife/article/20210615-how-the-salary-ask-gap-perpetuates-unequal-pay.

Romano, Benjamin, "Starbucks' CEO Compensation was 1,049 Times Greater than its Median Employee's," *Seattle Times*, January 29, 2019, https://www.seattletimes.com/business/starbucks/starbucks-ceos-compensation-was-1049-times-greater-than-its-median-employees/.

Romero, Anthony B., "In Memory of Justice Ruth Bader Ginsburg (1933–2010)," ACLU, September 18,

2020, https://www.aclu.org/news/civil-liberties/
in-memory-of-justice-ruth-bader-ginsburg-1933-2020.

Ronan, Wyatt, "New FBI Hate Crimes Report Shows Increases
in Anti-LGBTQ Attacks," Human Rights Campaign,
November 17, 2020, https://www.hrc.org/press-releases/
new-fbi-hate-crimes-report-shows-increases-in-anti-lgbtq-attacks.

Ross, John A., "The Reliability, Validity, and Utility of Self-Assessment,"
Practical Assessment, *Research & Evaluation* 11, no. 10 (November
2006): 1–13.

Sandel, Michael, *The Tyranny of Merit: What's Become of the Common
Good*, New York: Farrar, Strauss & Giroux, 2020.

Schneider, Mike, "Census Data: US Is Diversifying, White Population Shrinking," AP News, August 12, 2021, https://apnews.
com/article/race-and-ethnicity-census-2020-7264a653037e38df-
7ba67d3a324fc90d.

Sears, Brad et al., "LGBT People's Experience of Workplace Discrimination and Harassment," UCLA School of Law: Williams Institute,
September, 2021, https://williamsinstitute.law.ucla.edu/wp-content/
uploads/Workplace-Discrimination-Sep-2021.pdf.

Shane, Leo, "Here Are the Industries Where Veterans Are Finding Jobs,"
Military Times, April 21, 2022, https://www.militarytimes.com/
education-transition/2022/04/21/here-are-the-industries-where-
veterans-are-finding-jobs/#:~:text=As%20a%20percentage%20of%20
the,and%20health%20(9%25%20vs.

SHRM Foundation, "Join SHRM," SHRM Executive Network, accessed
July 30, 2022, https://shrm.org/pages/default.aspx.

Shroff, Amita, "Klinefelter Syndrome (XXY Syndrome)," WebMD,
September 22, 2021, https://www.webmd.com/men/
klinefelter-syndrome.

Southern Poverty Law Center, "Hate Group Tracker," SPLC, accessed July 28, 2022, https://www.splcenter.org/hate-map?ideology=anti-muslim.

Statista Research Department, "Population Distribution in the United States in 2020, by Generation," Statista, 2021, https://www.statista.com/statistics/296974/us-population-share-by-generation/.

Steinhauer, Jennifer, "Veterans Are Working, but Not in Jobs That Match Their Advanced Training," *New York Times*, March 7, 2020, https://www.nytimes.com/2020/03/07/us/politics/veterans-jobs-employment.html.

Sull, Donald, Charles Sull, and Ben Zweig, "Toxic Culture Is Driving the Great Resignation," *MIT Sloan Management Review*, January 11, 2022, https://sloanreview.mit.edu/article/toxic-culture-is-driving-the-great-resignation/.

Textio Editors, "Boost Your Talent Brand," Textio, accessed July 28, 2022, https://textio.com/products/.

The Friends, "Home," The Friends, accessed July 30, 2022, https://www.thefriends.on.ca/.

Trevor Project Editors, "Facts About LGBTQ Youth Suicide," The Trevor Project, accessed July 29, 2022, https://www.thetrevorproject.org/resources/article/facts-about-lgbtq-youth-suicide/.

Tsipursky, Gleb, *The Truth-Seeker's Handbook: A Science-Based Guide*, Columbus, Ohio: Intentional Insights Press, 2018.

United Negro College Fund, "The Numbers Don't Lie: HBCU's Are Changing the College Landscape," accessed July 28, 2022, https://uncf.org/the-latest/the-numbers-dont-lie-hbcus-are-changing-the-college-landscape.

United States Census Bureau, "2020 Census Frequently Asked Questions about Race and Ethnicity," Census.gov, August 12, 2021, https://www.census.gov/programs-surveys/decennial-census/decade/2020/planning-management/release/faqs-race-ethnicity.html.

United States Census Bureau, "2020 Census Statistics Highlight Local Population Changes and Nation's Racial and Ethnic Diversity," Census.gov, August 12, 2021, https://www.census.gov/newsroom/press-releases/2021/population-changes-nations-diversity.html.

Veterans Affairs, "Careers and Employment," US Department of Veteran Affairs, updated November 23, 2021, https://www.va.gov/careers-employment/.

Veterans Affairs, "National Veteran Suicide Prevention Annual Report," US Department of Veteran Affairs, September 2021, https://www.mentalhealth.va.gov/docs/data-sheets/2021/2021-National-Veteran-Suicide-Prevention-Annual-Report-FINAL-9-8-21.pdf.

Visconti, Luke, "Starbucks: Don't Close the Stores, Close Corporate Headquarters," DiversityInc, April 18, 2018.

Visram, Talib, "The Deep-Rooted Myth of Meritocracy Is Widening the Racial Wealth Gap," Maine Lobster Marketing Collaborative, October 4, 2021, https://socialequity.duke.edu/wp-content/uploads/2021/10/10.1.21.pdf

Walonick, David S., *Survival Statistics*, New York: StatPac Incorporated, 2013.

WICT Editors, "Let the WICT Network Be Your Guide in Diversifying Your Team," WICT Network, Accessed July 27, 2022, https://wict.org/diversity-facts-best-practices/.

Williams Institute, "LGBT FAQs," UCLA School of Law, accessed July 29, 2022, https://williamsinstitute.law.ucla.edu/quick-facts/lgbt-faqs/.

Williams, Walter L., "The 'Two-Spirit' People of Indigenous North Americans," *Guardian*, October 11, 2020, https://www.theguardian.com/music/2010/oct/11/two-spirit-people-north-america.

Wilson, Valerie, "Inequities Exposed: How COVID-19 Widened Racial Inequities in Education, Health, and the Workforce," Economic

Policy Institute, June 22, 2020, https://www.epi.org/publication/covid-19-inequities-wilson-testimony/.

"Women of Color in Management: Paying it Forward." *South Florida Business Journal*, June 30, 2022, accessed March 16, 2023, https://www.bizjournals.com/southflorida/news/2022/06/30/women-of-color-in-management-paying-it-forward.html.

World Health Organization Press Release, "Ageism Is a Global Challenge: UN," WHO, March 18, 2021, https://www.who.int/news/item/18-03-2021-ageism-is-a-global-challenge-un.

Young, Robin, "Name Discrimination Study Finds Lakisha and Jamal Still Less Likely to Get Hired than Emily and Greg," WBUR, August 18, 2021, https://www.wbur.org/hereandnow/2021/08/18/name-discrimination-jobs.

Zippia Editors, "Doctoral Student Demographics and Statistics in the US," Zippia, accessed July 28, 2022, https://www.zippia.com/doctoral-student-jobs/demographics/.

Zweigenhaft, Richie, "Fortune 500 CEOs, 2000-2020: Still Male, Still White," the Society Pages, October 28, 2020, accessed March 16, 2023, https://thesocietypages.org/specials/fortune-500-ceos-2000-2020-still-male-still-white/.

ACKNOWLEDGMENTS

Thank you to all who have supported diversity, equity and inclusion efforts in the US and around the world. Together, we are helping to move the needle toward a sense of belonging and justice for all. It is my hope that this book serves to help the effort in some small way.

Thank you to all the Spectra Diversity Change Partners who have taught me so much in our monthly meetings and ongoing relationships. The Spectra Partners have helped me to understand how to increase my interpersonal skills related to diversity, equity and inclusion while confirming and reconfirming my personal beliefs.

Thank you to those who agreed to share their very personal stories for inclusion in this book. Rebecca, Sonja, Ron, Robin, Max and Hank—your bravery is awesome.

A very special thank you to my colleagues who read all or portions of my book draft to correct any misconceptions I may have had and provide additional focus. This includes Lenora Billings-Harris; Amy Waninger; Julia Celeste Rosenfeld; Madonna Lennon; Nadege Minois, PhD; Greg Jenkins, CPTD; Duffy Pearce; Amanuel Medhanie, PhD; Dr. Kristen Liesch; Sandra Martinez, PhD; and Tawana Bhagwat. Your input and review were a critical part of the writing process.

Thank you to the staff at Advantage Books and especially my editor, Mel Sellick, who kept asking the questions that pushed me into thinking about the reader experience.

And lastly, thank you to my family, for keeping me grounded and grateful for life's travel and experiences; to my parents, who showed me how to live a long and healthy life; to my sister, who has shown me how to deal with difficult situations and still find time to laugh; and to my grandmother (my daughter's namesake) and her sister, who gave me unconditional love and forecast my future shortly after I was born. They said that I would have two dutiful children and find success as a writer.

www.ingramcontent.com/pod-product-compliance
Lightning Source LLC
Chambersburg PA
CBHW020527270326
41927CB00006B/482